WALKING IN
THE CHILTERNS

Statue and West Wycombe House. (Walk 19)

WALKING IN
THE CHILTERNS

by

DUNCAN UNSWORTH

CICERONE PRESS
MILNTHORPE, CUMBRIA

© Duncan Unsworth 1993
ISBN 1 85284 127 3

A catalogue record for this book is available from the British Library.

Photographs by the author

ACKNOWLEDGEMENTS

Many thanks must go to Lindsay for her company and for her judgement on many of the walks, as well as for her frequent help during the writing of this book.

Thanks must also go to Ian Head and particularly to John Sherlock for their diligence in checking route descriptions.

Finally for the help of Cicerone Press.

Advice to Readers

Readers are advised that whilst every effort is taken by the author to ensure the accuracy of this guidebook, changes can occur which may affect the contents. It is advisable to check locally on transport, accommodation, shops etc but even rights-of-way can be altered and, more especially overseas, paths can be eradicated by landslip, forest fires or changes of ownership.

The publisher would welcome notes of any such changes

Front Cover: Walking in bluebells above Dunscombe. (Walk 2)

CONTENTS

Introduction 9

Maps 11

Access 11

Geology 12

Natural history 14

History 16

Walk 1. Dunstable Downs - Whipsnade 20

Walk 2. Aldbury - Ivinghoe Beacon 23

Walk 3. Ashridge - Little Gaddesden 28

Walk 4. Potten End - Nettleden - Great Gaddesden 34

Walk 5. Gaddesden Place 37

Walk 6. Wendover - The Lee 40

Walk 7. Ellesborough - Dunsmore 45

Walk 8. Great Kimble - Whiteleaf Cross 49

Walk 9. Great Hampden - Little Hampden 52

Walk 10. Great Hampden - Lacey Green 58

Walk 11. Amersham - Great Missenden - Wendover 62

Walk 12. Cholesbury - Grim's Ditch 68

Walk 13. Hawridge 72

Walk 14. Chipperfield - Sarratt 76

Walk 15. Chenies - Latimer 80

Walk 16. Bledlow - Radnage 85

Walk 17. Bradenham - Lacey Green 89

Walk 18. West Wycombe - Bradenham 94

Walk 19. Wheeler End - Towerage 99

Walk 20. Penn - Forty Green 102

Walk 21. Coleshill - Winchmore Hill 107

Walk 22. Burnham Beeches - Littleworth Common 110

Walk 23. Fulmer - Hedgerley 114

Walk 24. Watlington Hill 119

Walk 25. Ibstone - Turville 122

Walk 26. Fingest - Skirmett - Turville 126

Walk 27. Turville Heath - Stonor 130

Walk 28. Hambleden Valley 134

Walk 29. Ewelme - Swyncombe 138

Walk 30. Nettlebed - Russell's Water 141

Walk 31. Nuffield 145

Walk 32. Henley-on-Thames - Fawley 147

Walk 33. Henley-on-Thames - Rotherfield Greys 152

Walk 34. Checkendon - Ipsden - Stoke Row 156

Walk 35. Goring - Whitchurch 161

Appendix A Other Chiltern walks 165

Appendix B Places to visit 167

Appendix C Public transport 168

Bibliography 169

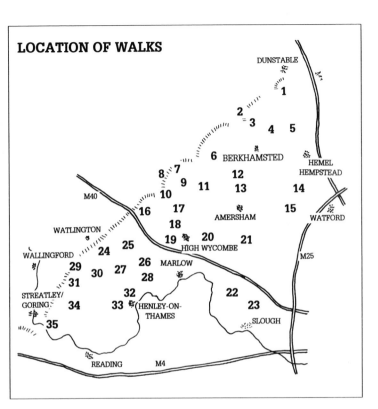

LOCATION OF WALKS

DUNSTABLE

1

2

3   4   5

6 BERKHAMSTED

HEMEL
HEMPSTEAD

8 7

12

9   11

13

14

M40

10

16   17

15

18

WATLINGTON

AMERSHAM

WATFORD

19   20   21

HIGH WYCOMBE

24   25

M25

WALLINGFORD

26 MARLOW

29   30   27   28

31

22

STREATLEY/
GORING

32

23

34   33 HENLEY-ON-
THAMES

SLOUGH

35

READING   M4

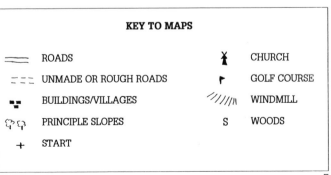

KEY TO MAPS

ROADS

CHURCH

UNMADE OR ROUGH ROADS

GOLF COURSE

BUILDINGS/VILLAGES

WINDMILL

PRINCIPLE SLOPES

S   WOODS

+   START

INTRODUCTION

The Chilterns are a band of chalk hills running north-east from the River Thames, in a swathe through the southern parts of Oxfordshire, Buckinghamshire, Hertfordshire and into a corner of Bedfordshire. Rising to 267 metres, they are by no means the highest hills in Britain but, even so, do possess a sense of grandeur with a dramatic scarp along the north-west edge overlooking the Oxfordshire plains and the Vale of Aylesbury. Away from the scarp the landscape is of a more intimate nature with woods, hedgerows, deep little valleys, charming villages, cosy pubs and old churches. Justifiably, the region has been designated an Area of Outstanding Beauty.

Within the Chilterns there is a particularly dense network of footpaths and bridleways totalling nearly 1000 miles. Using these public rights of way and permissive paths this guide describes thirty-five walks, of which all but one are circular. The exception, Walk 11 (between Amersham and Wendover), starts and finishes at stations on a railway line with a frequent service. The routes are designed not only to take in the best of the Chiltern landscape but also to visit the picturesque villages, old churches, and other historical curiosities. Distances of the walks vary between 5.6 and 18.3km (about $3^1/_2$ and $11^1/_2$ miles), the majority being half-day or gentle full-day walks.

In general the paths are well maintained and often signposted. Yellow and blue arrows are frequently used to mark footpaths and bridleways respectively, although white arrows are also used in many places. Increasingly the arrows are accompanied by a code of letters and numbers, the definitive map reference number, which are also shown on the Chiltern Society maps. The Chiltern Society deserves special praise for its work in protecting the public rights of way in the region. Unfortunately not all paths are clearly marked and, particularly in the beechwoods when the ground is covered in leaves, care may be needed not to lose the path. As the landscape is continually changing no doubt some details will have changed since the writing of this guide but common sense, and checking with maps, should prevail over any difficulties. Also, please do respect any revisions and diversions made to the rights of way.

With the increasing popularity of horse riding many of the

bridleways, and a number of the footpaths, are suffering. During wet weather the clay soils can soon become churned by horses into a very glutinous mud. Consequently, to be prepared, I would advise wearing walking boots or wellingtons except during dry periods. In summer, when the temperatures may advocate the wearing of shorts, is when the nettles are particularly vicious. So, unless, you wish to spend time delicately picking your way past the almost inevitable clump of nettles to avoid red blotchy legs, keep to long trousers. Apart from being prepared for mud and nettles there are few special problems but, although never far from civilization, it is always worth taking sensible footwear, clothing and sustenance to cope with the prevailing and possible weather conditions.

Refreshments can often be found at the many pubs in the area. These pubs are usually mentioned in the route descriptions but not all have been tested. Those I have tested have generally offered a very high standard of food, beer and hospitality adding an extra dimension to the enjoyment of the walk. Although some walks have enough pubs to become a pub-crawl - dipsomaniacs beware there is not a pub on every walk.

As with walking anywhere please follow the country code, in essence taking only photographs and leaving only footprints (and those only where appropriate). Many of the walks pass interesting old churches and descriptions are given of those normally open. When visiting these please remember that churches are not museums but places of living worship. Do not disturb services, make donations to help the cost of maintenance, remove boots rather than leave muddy footprints, and have a moment of prayer. Only by treating them with proper respect can we hope the churches remain open for all to see in the future. There has already been an incident at Great Hampden where someone, despite the fire hazard, was found brewing up on a pew and so the church, with its fine monument to John Hampden, is now kept locked.

MAPS

The maps included in the route descriptions are sketch maps, not drawn to scale, but designed to aid the user to trace the walk on official maps. The area is well covered, with three main options, the Ordnance Survey 1:50000 and 1:25000 maps and the Chiltern Society 1:25000 maps.

Ordnance Survey 1:50000 Landranger maps: 165, 166, 174*, 175.

Ordnance Survey 1:25000 Pathfinder maps: 1072 (TL02/12)*, 1094 (SP81/91), 1095 (TL01/11), 1117 (SP60/70)*, 1118 (SP80/90), 1119 (TL00/10), 1137 (SU69/79), 1138 (SU89/99), 1139 (TQ09/19), 1155 (SU48/58)*, 1156 (SU68/78), 1157 (SU88/98), 1171 (SU47/57)*

* *only covers a very short section of a walk.*

Chiltern Society Maps 1 to 20 cover most of the Chilterns but not Walks 1, 22 and 23. (No walk in this guide uses Map 1.)

The Chiltern Society maps are printed in black and white and thus lack some of the detail and intrinsic charm of the Ordnance Survey 1:25000 maps. They do however have the advantages of more recent revisions, showing the path numbers, and a couple of suggested walks on the back.

ACCESS

A number of rapid roads (the A423, M40, A413, and A41), radiating out from London pass through the region and although away from these the roads can soon become very countrified motorists should have no problems of access. Parking can occasionally be a problem but do remember to be considerate to others and particularly to locals.

Public transport is rather sporadic. The main towns and the Goring, Princes Risborough, Wendover, and Berkhamsted gaps are all on rail routes from London with frequent commuter train services. Beyond this some of the villages are on bus routes, but all too often bus services are very infrequent and non-existent on Sundays. Quite a few of the walks are totally inaccessible by public transport. The best walks for those using public transport are: 6, 11,

30, 32, 33, 35. I would strongly advise checking timetables of trains and buses before attempting any walk. (See phone numbers in Appendix B.)

GEOLOGY

During the Cretaceous period, 60 to 120 million years ago, what is now southern England was covered by sea. On the seabed shell detritus collected to form chalk, a soft white limestone of nearly pure calcium carbonate. The only impurity of any consequence was a small quantity of quartz, which since the initial formation of the chalk has been redistributed to form the now frequently found hard flints.

The chalk rose out of the sea, in a general trend sloping down from the north west, and was then folded as part of the outer ripples of the great tectonic activity that produced the Alps in Europe. To describe the Chilterns as foothills of the Alps may be stretching things a little too far. The Chilterns running along the north-west edge of the chalk form the lip of the London Basin. On one side, the chalk has been eroded to reveal the older greensands, whilst on the other side it dips gently beneath London, and a covering of younger gravels and clays before re-emerging as the North Downs. (See diagram.)

In deposited rocks bedding layers of different hardnesses are often found, and within the chalk the hardest layer is in the middle. Consequently along the north-west edge, where the chalk ends, a steep scarp has formed in the middle chalk. At the foot of the slope is the softer lower chalk bed above the greensands. The top and gentle dip slope are also formed from a softer layer, the upper chalk.

The Chilterns, however, are not just a uniform ridge with scarp and dip slopes but have been breached in several places to form blocks and gaps. The Goring gap, with the River Thames, is the most conspicuous and forms the divide from the Berkshire Downs. It is also the only gap with a substantial river to explain its creation. The others must have been formed by similar rivers, flowing from the north-west, which have now disappeared. A possible explanation is that during the last Ice Age a large lake was trapped by the ice to the north-west of the Chilterns and the gaps were cut by escaping water.

The dip slope of the Chilterns has numerous valleys but, as the chalk is permeable, water seeps down through it, and so very few streams can be found on the surface. The classic explanation for these dry valleys is that as the scarp slope has been eroded back the water table has dropped and the streams that cut the valleys were "captured" and now flow from the scarp slope. A better theory, though, is that during the last geologically cold period the ground was frozen, and hence impermeable, thus drainage had to be by surface streams which carved the now dry valleys.

Another feature of the Chilterns is the geologically recent deposits of clay found in many places and particularly around Nettlebed which was used for making bricks and tiles. Another result of the deposition of the clay has been to line hollows creating ponds in the most unlikely elevated positions.

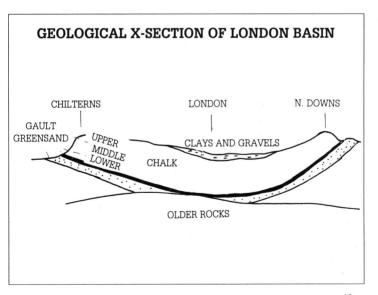

NATURAL HISTORY

As with most of the British Isles the geology and evolution is only the canvas which man has altered, sometimes subtly, at other times radically, to create the "natural" environment. In the Chilterns the result is a fine mosaic of different types of vegetation and ecosystems, an indication of which is that the area can boast more species of orchid and helleborines than any other similar sized area in Britain.

Beechwoods, the vegetation most closely associated with the Chilterns area, are one of the treasures of the area. These truly majestic trees have something to offer in every season: the translucent pale green leaves in spring; the shade in summer; the deep amber of the autumn leaves; and the rustle of dead leaves under foot during winter. Although the shade and deep leaf litter prevent all but the most determined undergrowth, some woods have the extra delight of a striking carpet of bluebells covering the floor in early summer. In the storms a few years ago some of the beechwoods were badly affected, leading to an increase in the amount of felling and replanting.

Although, due to its abundance, the beech is sometimes called "the Buckinghamshire weed" it is by no means the only species of tree in the area. Ancient oaks can be found in the Ashridge Estate and the misnamed Burnham Beeches. Elsewhere mixed woodlands are common, with oak, beech, ash, sycamore, wild cherry, holly, yew, and hornbeam being among the species found there. The trees are often shrouded with streamers of a wild clematis, sometimes called Travellers Joy or Old Mans Beard. Plantations of larch and spruce are also widespread throughout the Chilterns. The older plantations tend to be deserts for other living species, but the Chiltern Project, started in 1951 by the Forestry Commission, has done much to create a better balance between the aesthetic and commercial aspects of forestry.

The open land in the Chilterns can also be divided into several categories, the largest of which is mixed arable and pasture farmland. Fortunately the contours of the land have prevented the vast scale mechanisation so often seen on flatter agricultural land. Consequently many, but by no means all, of the old hedgerows have been retained, providing a valuable habitat for wildlife.

Downland, with springy turf and an abundance of wild flowers, is also common, particularly along the edge of the scarp, such as at Watlington Hill, Ivinghoe Beacon and Dunstable Downs (Walks 24, 2 and 1). In many places this downland is beginning to revert towards a mixed woodland, being first colonised by hawthorns which give protection to non-thorny bushes like elder and then eventually to Wild Cherry, Whitebeam, and other small trees.

The other main forms of open ground are heaths and commons. These are often found on the more acidic soils which have formed on old river terraces or fluvio-glacial deposits. The best examples are at Stoke Common, Turville Common and Russell's Water Common (Walks 23, 27 and 30). Typically the vegetation of these includes silver birch trees, gorse and bracken.

Numerous varieties of birds frequent the varied habitats of the Chilterns. In the beechwoods a particular delight is the greater spotted woodpecker which makes its presence known, during spring, with a rapid knocking noise. Other birds to be found in the woodlands include: nuthatch, wood warbler, chaffinch, goldcrest, jay and various tits. The open areas tend to be inhabited by the more airborne species such as kestrels and the skylarks which are often heard in summer. However the noisiest bird to inhabit the region must be the pheasant whose harsh call frequently disturbs the peace.

Mammals of the region include foxes and badgers although most commonly seen (or rather heard as they shyly run off into the woodland undergrowth) are deer. As game for the estates, deer have always been important and when the Stonor family owned two houses in the Chilterns the deer were moved, like other possessions, to whichever house was occupied at the time. Fallow deer are the most widespread although roe deer are reappearing in the south and the diminutive muntjac, which was brought to Woburn in 1890, has escaped and been seen in the northern Chilterns. Another escapee, apparently now at home in the Chesham area, is the fat or edible dormouse, first introduced into Tring Park by Walter Rothschild in 1902.

HISTORY

Although early man probably hunted in the Chilterns it was only during the Neolithic period (3000 to 1800BC) that he first began to alter the environment. Farmers, living in semi-permanent settlements, started using slash and burn methods to clear the natural vegetation, which was then hindered from regrowing by their livestock. The actions of these early farmers was, however, quite limited in the region due to a combination of the clay soils, which were too heavy for early implements, and the lack of water on the chalk. Indeed the lack of water has remained a problem and until just pre-war, with the advent of the mains water supply, collection tanks, ponds and a few deep wells were the only source.

The greatest Neolithic achievement in the region was the creation of The Icknield Way, the first "road" in the country. This connected two main centres of Neolithic occupation, at Thetford in the Brecklands of the Little Ouse Basin and at Avebury in Wiltshire, as well as passing other commercial concerns such as the flint mines at Grime's Graves. Using the lie of the land this followed the scarp along the Chilterns, keeping above the spring line on the easier drier ground, and is now called the Upper Icknield Way. Until relatively recently the road would have been more a belt of turf than the track found in places today (eg. Walk 24). The Icknield Way was further developed during the subsequent Bronze and Iron Ages, later becoming a route for Saxons, Vikings, and other tribal invaders as well as for droving herds. With time, a chain of settlements associated with the Icknield Way grew at the bottom of the Chiltern scarp, where water was available, and a second route, the Lower Icknield Way, evolved between these villages.

Farming activity continued through the Bronze Age (1800 to 550BC) and numerous round barrows from the period can still be seen in the region. Most are now found along the top of the scarp, although this may reflect subsequent agricultural activity with others lost by the action of ploughs. During the Iron Age (550BC to AD43) hillforts came into vogue and there is evidence of several in the Chilterns, such as at Ivinghoe Beacon and Cholesbury (Walks 2 and 12).

The largest relic of early man in the Chilterns is Grim's Ditch, which was described by Massingham as "the longest serpent of antiquity". It originally ran for about 80km (50 miles) from the River Thames near Wallingford, up past Nuffield towards Henley and then from near Marlow behind the scarp past Lacey Green, Great Hampden, Berkhamsted and on to Ivinghoe Beacon and Dunstable. The ditch can still be seen in many places, particularly on Walks 2, 10, 12 and 31.

Many people have tried to explain who organised the large effort required to dig the ditch, and why. Pevsner assigns it a Saxon origin, as the eastern boundary of lands captured by Cuthwulf in 571. King Offa, who is known to have had a ditch dug along the border with Wales and had grounds within the Chilterns, is another candidate a couple of centuries later. Others have suggested it was built by Britons as a defence against the Danes, to stop cattle raids, as a boundary marker or even as a fire break.

As it seems the Saxons gave it the name of Grim's Ditch, attributing it to the Devil, and as there is no record of the Romans building it, logic would suggest that the ditch dates from Pre-Roman times. Recent excavations, by the Hertfordshire Archaeological Trust, have indeed dated the ditch as fourth century BC and suggest it originally had a 10ft high and 20ft wide bank, possibly with a wooden palisade, fronted by a 8ft and a 17ft wide ditch. They propose that the ditch was a frontier to an Iron Age tribe based at Synodun hill fort near Dorchester on the Oxford Plain. Running in front of a series of forts the ditch also served to protect the Icknield Way, which must have been a valuable asset to the tribe but was vulnerable lying beneath the wooded Chilterns. If this latest evidence is correct then Grim's Ditch is the longest prehistoric earthwork in Britain.

The Romans made little impact upon the Chilterns although remains of villas have been found in the Hambleden, Chess and Gade valleys. It is probably no coincidence that these three valleys are among the few with flowing water.

Only during the early Norman period were the Chilterns properly settled, although even then considerable woodlands were kept to provide fuel, foraging for animals and hunting grounds. Manors were created which formed the basis of later grand estates such as at Stonor and Ashridge. The Norman manors, for purposes of judicial administration and defence, were grouped into areas of "hundreds" with the Hundreds of Desborough, Burnham and Stoke forming the Chiltern Hundreds. At one time the Stewardship of the Chiltern Hundreds was an important position in trying to secure the area from the thieves and highwaymen who attacked the roads to Oxford and the north from the hills and woods. In reality the post no longer exists but with delightful idiosyncrasy Parliament still imagines it does. Today the only way for a Member of Parliament to resign honourably is to apply for the position of Steward of the Chiltern Hundreds, which if it existed would be an paid civic office and hence bar the person from being a MP.

Soon the growing settlements started to build churches and many Chiltern churches have a Norman origin. Two particularly fine but contrasting examples of this Norman architecture can be found at Swyncombe and Fingest (Walks 29 and 26). During the Middle Ages many of the churches were either rebuilt or extended and embellished. Typically this included the inside being painted with murals, which were then white-washed over during the the puritanical Cromwellian era. Several of these murals have been re-discovered, often in the 1930s, and can be seen at Little Missenden, Sarratt, Radnage, and Checkendon (Walks 11, 15, 16, and 34.) Another common feature of the churches is their frequent isolation. Several of the Chiltern villages, such as Little Gaddesden, Sarratt, Radnage, Ibstone, and Bix, have migrated for various reasons (such as to better water supplies or away from old plague infested centres) leaving the church, which was once in the centre of the village, now isolated.

In a seemingly bizarre piece of administration, during the Middle Ages, the Chilterns were part of the diocese of Lincoln. The region, however, has never been particularly conformist and during the 1400s and early 1500s Lollards, who objected to the bureaucracy of the church, were common. Unfortunately this led to several being martyred at Amersham for their beliefs. Later the Chilterns became important in the development of Quakerism, with William Penn coming from the village of that name (Walk 20) and who, together with other founders, is buried at Jordans near Chalfont St Peter.

The spirit of rebellion found in the Chilterns meant that the region had to play its part in the Civil War. In particular John Hampden, who lived at Hampden House (Walk 9), was one of the instigators of the rebellion. During the war he was killed at Chalgrove, at the foot of the Chilterns, whilst his son was killed at Chennies in another of the skirmishes that occurred in the area.

With few natural resources for industry the Chilterns is a largely agricultural region. Some small scale and cottage industries did exist such as straw platting, which spread to nearby Chiltern villages from Luton after being introduced there by James I. Also, evidence can still be seen at Nettledbed of the brick and tile industry that used the local clays, and wood for fuel. The main resource of the area, beechwood, did enable High Wycombe to develop as an important furniture making centre. Even this had a form of village counterpart with the bodgers. Until the 1930s bodgers could be found in many of the small villages where, working on simple pole lathes, they made chair legs which were then sold to the furniture factories.

Today, with the roads and railways crossing the region, the Chilterns is within commuting distance of London. Despite being in the Green Belt this has led to pressures for more homes in the area. A recent tendency has been to convert, not always appropriately, old black barns into houses. Increased leisure has also lead to pressures with a burgeoning of riding stables and a rash of new golf courses. The region does, however, have its own Chiltern Society, founded in 1965, both to act and to stimulate public awareness about the need to maintain the beauty and character of the Chiltern Hills.

WALK 1
Dunstable Downs - Whipsnade
(8.8km, 5¹/₂ miles)

MAPS: O.S. 1:25,000 Pathfinder Sheets 1095, 1072* and 1094
       O.S. 1:50,000 Landranger Sheets 165 and 166
       Not covered by Chiltern Society Footpath Map.
       (* only for very short distance)

Dunstable Downs form an outlier at the northern end of the Chiltern scarp and, being close to Dunstable and Luton, the top is a popular viewpoint for appreciating the scenery, and to watch the gliders from the London Gliding Club below. On Good Friday, Dunstable Downs traditionally are the scene of the strange custom of rolling oranges down the slope, to recall the rolling away of the stone from Christ's tomb.

This walk descends the edge of the down before following the quieter base of the scarp, where the un-grazed wild flowers attract many different butterflies. Returning to the top the walk then passes through the unusual and tranquil Whipsnade Tree Cathedral at the edge of that village's green.

START (008,198): There is a large car park and picnic area on the top of Dunstable Downs by the B4541 from Dunstable.

PUBLIC TRANSPORT: The walk can be joined at the grassy area between rows of sycamores by the junction of the B489 and B4541 about 1.3km from the centre of Dunstable. Buses between Luton and Hemel Hempstead (from Luton only on Sundays) also stop at Whipsnade village green.

ROUTE: From the visitor centre and toilets, start to drop down the scarp to a fence and turn right beside it along a path marked with yellow arrows and 'CR'. This follows the edge of the down with sweeping panoramic views to Ivinghoe Beacon and across the

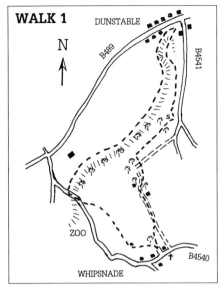

plains. Beyond a gate to more open downland, the path swings left onto a prominent spur and then bends right again to descend a ridge. *The mounds passed are Five Knolls, a group of tumuli, which were excavated in 1928 to reveal a fine Early Bronze period burial now on display in Luton Museum. Also unearthed were later Saxon skeletons who had their arms behind their backs, victims of the gallows which then stood upon the site.* Descend through the gate overlooking Dunstable, the junction of the Roman Watling Street and the older Icknield Way, towards a grassy area, between two rows of sycamore trees, leading towards a road.

Turn left and back onto a path by the first sycamore, and into trees beside the fence at the back of gardens. Through a gate, bend round the bottom of the spur and then down to the right, through bushes, to follow the base of the scarp by the fence of a field and then the London Gliding Club. Keep along the bottom, ignoring all paths off to the left, eventually to enter National Trust land and later reach a road.

Climb uphill for a few metres and then take the bridleway on the left, turning right by a gate to go up by the fence. Near the top the White Lion of Whipsnade, cut in 1933 to the design of R.B.Brooke-Greaves, can be seen on the scarp, to the right, below the wild animal park sited on land bought from the Ashridge estate. At the top go straight on along the bridleway, signposted to Whipsnade, through bushes. A path joins from the left by a grassy patch, keep on to the left corner and follow the main path through more bushes, and then

Base of Dunstable Downs

between hedges. After some distance this leads to a bungalow, and turn left at the junction beyond it and over the stile into National Trust land. Follow the edge of the field leading ahead and round to the right to a stile into an area of grass and trees, the Whipsnade Tree Cathedral. *Now owned by the National Trust the trees and hedges were laid out in a plan, inspired by Liverpool Cathedral, by Edmund Kell Blyth in the 1930s to commemorate three friends killed in 1918 in an unusual, but delightfully peaceful, form of remembrance contrasting with the anguish of the First World War.* Exit, either via the north entrance by the north trancept off the nave or ahead and slightly right along an avenue of younger trees to a car park with Whipsnade village green and the Chequers Inn beyond.

At the entrance to the car park a bridleway is signposted back to the left. This soon splits either side of a hedge to rejoin after the north entrance, and bend right to a road. Turn left along the road and past the Swallowsprings development of large modern houses to enter trees beyond a "no motors" sign. Keep on along the main track, passing the gate to Evergreen Lodge. By the mast, drop down to continue ahead beside the hedge on the right and then, across a small road, go ahead to a gate at the edge of the downs. Drop down most of the field before turning right along a bridleway to a gate. A clear route leads through hawthorn bushes to more open land where, along and to the right, is the visitor centre.

WALK 2
Aldbury - Ivinghoe Beacon
(12.3km,7³/₄ miles)

MAPS: O.S. 1:25,000 Pathfinder Sheet 1094
O.S. 1:50,000 Landranger Sheet 165
Chiltern Society Footpath Map No. 19

Ivinghoe is well known principally for two reasons. The first is due to Sir Walter Scott who after visiting the village altered the name for the title of his book, *Ivanhoe*. The second is Beacon Hill, or Ivinghoe Beacon as it is often called, standing above the village which is the end of the Ridgeway long distance footpath. Beacon Hill and nearby Pitstone Hill are some of the best areas of downland in the Chilterns. This walk starts by following the Ridgeway up Pitstone Hill passing a few remnants of Grim's Ditch. It also ends by descending along the Ridgeway from Beacon Hill and above the dramatically deep Incombe Hole. In between, the walk goes to the charming village of Aldbury with its black and white buildings, pond and stocks. Climbing into the woods of the Ashridge Estate it then passes the tall Doric column of the Bridgewater Monument and along the edge of a scarp to Beacon Hill.

START (955,149): The car park on the minor road between Pitstone and Aldbury, which leaves the B488 at a right-angled bend near the windmill. The car park is on the west side of the road below the end of the ridge of Pitstone hill and Aldbury Nowers.

It is equally possible to start the walk from Aldbury, the National Trust monument car park off the B4506 near Ashridge or the car parks by Ivinghoe Beacon. The reason for the suggested start is to give the walk the best balance and to leave the Beacon until near the end.

PUBLIC TRANSPORT: Buses run to Aldbury from Hemel Hempstead, Berkhapsted and Tring station (trains from London) but not on Sundays. Join the walk in the centre of the village.

ROUTE: From the stile, at the back of the car park, go diagonally to the left and then along the edge of the field and uphill past a section of Grim's Ditch. The summit of Pitstone hill is above a large chalk quarry but is nevertheless still a good viewpoint. At the corner, drop slightly over the edge and along by the remains of Grim's Ditch, to a stile into private woods. A good clear path leads through the pleasant woods, to a series of steps leading down to a junction of paths by a cross-section of Grim's Ditch.

Turn left, up the path for about 25 metres, and then fork right on a path along the top end of a small open patch of felled trees. Follow the path, near the left-hand edge of mixed woods and replanting, to beside a large fallen tree trunk and out to the edge of a golf course. (At the time of writing the golf course was being constructed over the next section and so some of the details may have changed, but hopefully the owners will mark the path adequately.) Go beside the trees and bushes of the

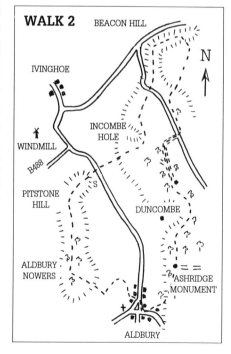

WALK 2

BEACON HILL

N

IVINGHOE

INCOMBE HOLE

WINDMILL

B488

PITSTONE HILL

S

DUNCOMBE

ALDBURY NOWERS

ASHRIDGE MONUMENT

ALDBURY

Aldbury village pond and Old Manor

old hedgerow ahead to their end. Past the base of an old tree, with a yellow arrow, continue down ahead towards the village, passing a little to the right of wooden power post, and on to a stile at the edge of course.

Turn left, along the bridleway, which can be muddy, leading between hedges to pass an old black and white signpost where a footpath joins from the left. Continue until just past a stile and gate on the left and look for a gap in the hedge to the right, between hawthorn and holly trees, leading to a stile. (This may be overgrown and if missed continue on to the road and turn right to the village.) Over the stile go diagonally to the left past a protruding corner of hedges and on between two large trees, from where there is a good profile view of Aldbury church with its oversized tower. Continue on to a stile near the corner of a wooden fence. Cross the school sports field to a stile at the opposite corner and follow the drive to the village by The Greyhound pub.

Although a Roman road may have passed through the area of the village, Aldbury was really settled in the Saxon times. The Saxon name

25

meant "*old fortified place*", although where these fortifications were is now a mystery. Today the buildings at the core of the village range from the early-sixteenth century to Victorian times. Perhaps the finest of the older buildings, if only for its prime position in front of the village pond, is the Old Manor House. This was never a proper manor house but the home of yeoman farmers, before being divided into smaller homes. A short perambulation along Stocks Road and then in the other direction to the church is well worth it if time allows. Like most of the Chiltern villages Aldbury was never a wealthy place and at one time relied on the cottage industry of straw plaiting to supplement the income from agriculture. Charity provided the three almshouses on Stocks Road, where in 1841 fifteen people lived. The small single-storey section was once a single roomed cottage in itself.

The church of St John the Baptist has a magnificent tower and aisles dating from the early-fourteenth century. The Pendley Chapel, inside the church, has a finely carved altar tomb depicting Sir Robert Whittingham, who died in 1471, and his wife.

Turn right, past the village pond, and then left up Toms Hill Road, before forking left onto a track opposite Netherby. After passing the backs of a few houses this enters the woods and climbs the scarp in a trench. A footpath joins from the right near the top and continues straight on, to an opening with the Bridgewater Monument and National Trust shop. (See Walk 3 for a history of Ashridge and the Bridgewaters.)

From the Bridgewater Monument take the bridleway ahead (signposted as a nature trail), across the road leading to some cottages, to keep along above the slope. Go straight on, past the "footpath only - no horses" sign, and on through the wood to cross a ditch by a small bridge. A bridleway joins from the right and then keep to the main track, passing above the remains of old chimneys in a clearing. As the level path leads round above Dunscombe gaps in the beechwoods, due to storm damage, give views across to the hill of Aldbury Nowers. At a forked junction keep straight on, and past a plantation of conifers, to the head of Dunscombe and a gap with views to Aldbury village. Curve left, round another plantation, and into a large beechwood with some sycamores. Continue on, past a cross-junction of paths, and along to be joined on the left by the field of Clipper Down. Go past the brick house to a gate and then

Approaching Beacon Hill

straight on along the unmade road descending in a cutting to a Y-junction, taking the higher right-hand road. Keep following the unmade road which bends to the right and goes past a bridleway, off to the left, before going over the top of the ridge to a car park by a road and a view of the lion carved in the chalk at Whipsnade.

Turn left and look for a path running in the strip of beeches on the right-hand side of the road leading to another large car park. This is the main car park for Beacon Hill and most of its users follow the footpath, signposted "To Ridgeway", from the end of the car park and round the head of the bowl to the summit. However a more attractive route is to follow the permissive paths, shown on the Chiltern Society maps, across the bottom of the bowl to approach the summit via the ridge from the other end. To do this, cross the stile on the right, a little before the path from the end of the car park, and drop down the steep slope, aiming towards the radio masts at the end of the ridge across the bowl. At the bottom corner of the field, near a water-trough, cross the stile by a gate and follow the green track along the edge of the field ahead. Then continue straight on along the track between two fields to their end and turn left up to a stile by a gate and on up beside a fence to the crest of the ridge. Turn left up along the gently climbing ridge. Looking back down the ridge is the mound of Gallows Hill, with views across to

Dunstable Down and Edlesbourgh Church. Cross the stile to reach the trig-point and summit of Beacon Hill which marks the end of the Ridgeway. *The hill is the site of a pear-shaped hilltop fort which has been dated as being built about 700BC. Apart from these earthworks there is also the worn down remains of a barrow a few metres to the south of the trig-point.*

Although rather dwarfed by the cement works, Pitstone windmill can be seen from the summit. A date of 1627 has been found inscribed on the windmill which would make it the oldest in the country, however also inscribed is the date of 1749. It may be the mill was built at this later date but using some timbers from an earlier mill. Normally with a postmill, like Pitstone mill, the body of the mill was turned on the post to face the wind, however in 1902 a freak storm caught the mill from behind. The sails were blown forward and spun the wrong way causing bearings to fly through the roof. Never working commercially again the mill was given in 1937 to the National Trust, who have restored it.

Turn left at the summit to follow the very worn path down to the road. Take the Ridgeway signposted ahead along a worn path but soon crossing a stile on the right to follow a footpath uphill through hawthorn bushes. Cross the stile and go up the left-hand side of the field with acorn signs indicating the route through hawthorns and gorse. The footpath then leads round the head of the very deep Incombe Hole, which even has some small scree slopes. Go round and down on a feint grassy footpath to cross a stile and pass between fields down to the road at the start of the walk.

WALK 3
Ashridge - Little Gaddesden
(11.3km, 7 miles or 7km, 4¹/₂ miles)

MAPS: O.S. 1:25,000 Pathfinder Sheets 1094 and 1095
O.S. 1:50,000 Landranger Sheets 165 and 166
Chiltern Society Footpath Map No. 19

This walk is largely within the old Ashridge Estate passing through

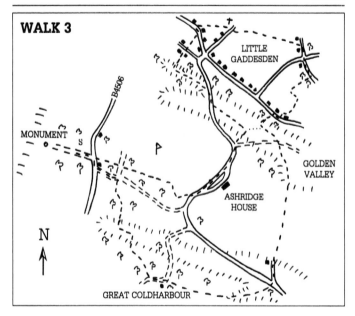

WALK 3

LITTLE
GADDESDEN

B4506

MONUMENT

GOLDEN
VALLEY

ASHRIDGE
HOUSE

N

GREAT COLDHARBOUR

old woods, along a grand avenue, past the extravagant house, into the aptly named Golden Valley whose long grass takes on a velvet sheen in late summer, and to the isolated Little Gaddesden Church overlooking the Gade Valley. The walk can be easily shortened, missing the church, giving two optional distances.

The Ashridge Estate dates back to the crusades when Edmund Crouchback, Earl of Cornwall, a nephew of King Henry III, created a deer-park out of the forest and built a palace for himself and a monastery for twenty monks of the order of Bon Hommes. It was the job of the monks to guard a golden box containing a few drops of Christ's blood brought by Edmund's father from the Patriarch of Jerusalem during the crusades. This relic soon made the monastery an important destination for pilgrims.

With the dissolution of the monasteries by Henry VIII, the relic was exposed as a fake, and the estate became a home for Henry's children. When Elizabeth became queen, however, she left it for good and sold it a few years later to Sir Thomas Egerton, the Lord Keeper of the Seal. The now enlarged estate remained in the Egerton family for three centuries as they took the titles of Earl, then Duke of Bridgewater, and later Earl Brownlow.

Francis Egerton, the Third Duke of Bridgewater, was a rather eccentric character, who among other things enjoyed the destruction of flowers and after being deserted by his fiancée, became an extreme misogynist. However, with the aid of James Brindley, an untutored but naturally gifted engineer, he fulfilled an idea of the First Duke's with the building of a canal in 1761 between the families' coal mines in Worsley, and Manchester. This was a great commercial success, halving the cost of coal, and heralded the boom in canal building, an important step in the industrial revolution. Although the most famous member of his family, it is ironic that the Duke should be commemorated by the prominent 108ft tall monument here, for he had little time for Ashridge and allowed it to fall into ruin.

The Duke's cousin and heir set about the rebuilding with the architect James Wyatt. The resultant Neo-Gothic mansion has variously been described as "a wedding cake", or "a forest of white spires and towers", and remains a striking and extravagant piece of architecture.

In 1921, upon the death of the Third Earl Brownlow, the estate was sold and is now largely in the ownership of the National Trust, apart from the house and immediate grounds, which belong to the Ashridge Management College.

START (979,128): The National Trust monument car park off the B4506 near Ashridge. Charge payable at weekends in the summer. Park close to the entrance unless visiting the monument, shop, exhibition or toilets which are open every day between April and October except Fridays.

PUBLIC TRANSPORT: Buses from Hemel Hempstead and Berkhamsted (not Sundays) can be taken to the Bridgewater Arms in Little Gaddesden, part way through the longer walk.

ROUTE: Return to the road and go through the gate in the dip opposite. Head towards Ashridge House, in the distance at the end of the long avenue of Princes Riding, until it is barred by a fence at the edge of a golf fairway. Turn right before the fence, on a footpath leading behind a tree with a seat, to a junction with a horse track and turn left along this, in the trees around the back of the green. Fork right, shortly, at a Y-junction in bracken and, keeping right again, go

Bridgewater Monument

through the trees on a track to meet a road.

Turn left along the road, beside the playing fields, in front of the college grounds to the toll booth of this private road. (Pedestrians are currently free of charge.) Ahead, at the bend in the road, an opening in the trees forms a vista across the Golden Valley to a cross, built to commemorate Adelaide (1844 - 1917) the wife of Adelbert, 3rd Earl Brownlow. Descend through the opening to the valley and turn left to follow it for the longer walk. (Turn right for the shorter walk to rejoin the route at (A) below in the description.)

Reaching the road, turn right to where the trees meet the road on the right, and there is a wide track in the trees opposite, and continue a few metres further up the road to find a small path which veers off to the left, between a hawthorn and an oak tree. Follow this along the floor of a quiet and largely wooded valley. After some distance, the path runs beside garden fences to a junction. Turn right, between hedges, and up past a drive to a minor road. Almost opposite, the path continues between fences to a stile and into the car park of The Bridgewater Arms free house.

Turn left along the road, past this elegant Georgian building, to a bend where a footpath is signposted right through the gate before October House. Cross the field diagonally to the right, to a stile, and continue in the same direction across the next field and then beside the wire fence of a third field, to a gate and sight of the church. Go straight on, across the field, to a gate and road beside the churchyard.

Despite fragments dating from the fifteenth century the appearance of the church, St Peter and St Paul, is largely Victorian. The main interest, however, is the inside, lavishly adorned with monuments commemorating the Egerton family. Despite the Dukes and Earls remembered here one of the most charming monuments is to Elizabeth Dutton, grand-daughter of Sir Thomas Egerton, and was only moved to here, from St Martin-in-the-Fields, in 1730 when the church there was demolished. Elizabeth died, broken-hearted, within a year of her husband being tragically killed in a fall from the horse they were riding together after their wedding.

Another interesting monument is that to Francis Henry, the eighth Earl of Bridgewater and another of the family's eccentrics, whose many dogs and cats ate at the table with him, dressed like people. In his will he bequeathed £8000 for the writing of essays, 'to prove the benevolence of God as displayed in the works of Creation'. Among those contributing essays was Roget, the author of Roget's Thesaurus.

Cross the stile opposite the church gate, and turn left immediately along by the fence and then straight on across the field to a stile in hawthorn trees. The views reveal the true position of the church, above the Gade Valley. Over the stile, follow the left-hand edge of the long field. At the end, continue straight on, over the stile to a gate by a beech hedge, and then to the road.

Turn right, and cross the main road to follow the small road opposite. Past Hudnall Farm there is a large opening on the left, overlooking the Gade Valley, and part way along this a bridleway is signposted into the trees on the right. This then leads between fences, bending left then right, across a shallow valley to the buildings of the Home Farm, at the edge of Little Gaddesden. Turning right, in front of a wall, and then left, through a gate, go down between fences to the drive and then to the road.

Turn right along the pavement until, shortly past the drive to The Bothy, a footpath is signposted into the bushes across the road. A tarmac path then leads down to the Golden Valley again and once

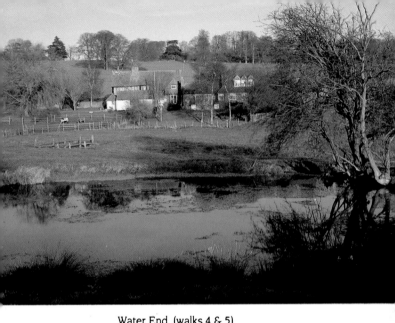

Water End (walks 4 & 5)
Great Kimble Church (walk 8)

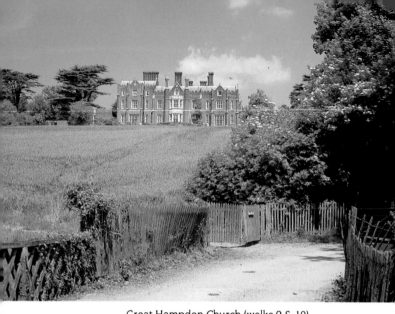

Great Hampden Church (walks 9 & 10)
Latimer House (walk 15)

there turn left.

(A) Go along the valley to meet a gravel track, and across this, a very faint path contours round to a gate and stile in a wooden fence. The path continues, leading through an isolated group of three beech trees, and on to a stile at the top. Go along, between the wire fences, to join the road from Rodinghead and straight down to the road at the bottom.

Cross this road and take the bridleway into the trees on the right. This soon leads to a junction, at the corner of open ground. Keep straight on, between trees and the open ground, along a valley. At the junction at the end, veer right along a track into the trees. Soon keep right, at a junction with more tracks, to reach another junction, in front of Great Coldharbour.

Go straight on, along the gravel track ahead, a short distance, to a left bend and leave it here on an un-marked path leading straight on into the trees. This soon becomes a green track, which is very boggy in places, but is also accompanied by a drier path. Pass a couple of junctions with barely distinguishable green paths but then, as the ground becomes more open but bracken filled to the right, look for a solitary birch tree in the middle of the green track. This marks another cross-junction. Turn right here, along a path through the bracken, and keep going down to the bottom.

Turn left, along the bridleway, beside a row of large beech trees to the end of open ground to the right, and then turn right up a path by another row of beech trees. By the corner of the field to the right, keep straight on, but now to the right of the row of beech trees. The path leads to the right of a small pond, and then bends left a little, through birch and bracken, to join a track. Go to the right, beside this, to a junction and turn left along the small road to meet the B4506, by the chequered stone-and-flint Thunderdell Lodge. A short distance to the right, along the road, is the entrance to the Monument Car Park.

WALK 4
Potten End - Nettleden - Great Gaddesden
(10km, 6¹/₄ miles)

MAPS: O.S. 1:25,000 Pathfinder Sheets 1095 and 1119
O.S. 1:50,000 Landranger Sheet 166
Chiltern Society Footpath Map No. 20

Potten End is situated on the high ground above Berkhamsted. Although much of the village is relatively modern it does retain an attractive village green and pond. At one time the locals had a reputation for leaving their doors open in the hope that sheep, being driven along the turnpike, would stray inside.

Dropping down to the attractive hamlet of Frithsden, the walk then crosses the folds in the land towards the larger Gade Valley. The farmland in the area tends to be open with few hedgerows. Although this may not sound so good it does give one a chance to appreciate the beauty of the basic shape of the land and gives the walk a distinctive feel. From Great Gaddesden and the water meadows at Water End, below the grand Gaddesden Place, the walk returns via woodland and more open farmland.

START (017,088): Parking by green opposite the Village Hall, Potten End.

PUBLIC TRANSPORT: Potten End is on a bus route between Hemel Hempstead and Berkhamsted (not Sundays).

ROUTE: Go down the road between the brick church and the school to a crossroads. Continue straight ahead along Plough Lane, past the Plough Inn, but then where the road bends left towards houses continue straight on the track, signposted to Nettleden, past allotments. At the entrance to Brown Springs Farm cross a couple of stiles to the field beyond. Follow the edge by a wood to a stile and then down to the bottom right corner of the next field and a stile to a bridleway. Turn left along the bridleway from where Gaddesden

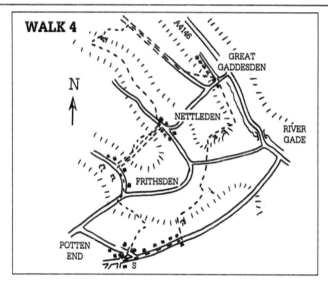

Place, prominent above a valley, can be seen in the distance and continue down to a road.

Turn right a few metres along the road to a junction and take the left fork, signposted towards Frithsden. *The village, once surrounded by orchards, was renowned for its fine black cherries and every year held a cherry festival. Today cherries seem to have been replaced by drink.* Immediately past The Alford Arms, which has its own brew-house, turn right down the side of a small triangular green, with trees, in front of the ornate Little Manor. Follow the narrow road, climbing between cottages and past the Frithsden Vineyard, out of the valley. From the summit both Ashridge House, in the distance along the ridge on the left, and Gaddesden Place, ahead, can be seen. Cross the second of two stiles, on the left at the top, and follow the hedge parallel to the track down. This gives good views of the area including a gentle valley with a solitary tree, the route out of Nettleden. Cross a couple of stiles by a bridge over the track and continue straight on down to another stile to re-join the road down to the bottom and a junction in Nettleden.

The main part of the village, a church and a few pleasant

cottages, is just to the right along the road, however, turn left and then very shortly off to the right on a footpath, signposted to Great Gaddesden, beneath power cables. At the end of the hedge on the left turn left and follow the path ahead in the field to a solitary tree. The path then follows the wide and dry valley bottom round to a clump of shrubs, hiding what was once a pond, where the valley bends to the left. Continue along the base of the valley until, shortly beyond the next copse on the right-hand slope above, a marker post usually marks a junction of paths. Turn right and leave the valley floor passing a few metres behind the copse. At the top, with views down the valley and over to Potten End, bend diagonally to the right at a junction of fields which is barely noticeable unless contrasting crops are being grown.

On the summit the path reaches a road by a small pond surrounded by oak trees. Turn right along the initially un-made road following the crest of a wide ridge. Near the end of a compound of wooden dormitories, the Amarvavati Buddhist Centre, there is a stile and footpath, signposted to Great Gaddesden, on the left of the road next to a small track. Descend, following the edge of the field next to a wood, to a stile and into an area of rough pasture with no obvious path. Keep to the same direction and through one of the holes in a hedge at the other side and down to the bottom right corner of the field and a stile into the churchyard of St John the Baptist, Great Gaddesden. *The church has an outward Victorian appearance but some of the fabric is much older, including some bricks re-cycled from a nearby Roman villa. A chapel and a number of monuments are dedicated to the Halsey family who owned Gaddesden Place (see Walk 5).*

Out of the the main gate at the bottom of the churchyard, turn right along a small road to a T-junction by The Cock and Bottle pub. Almost opposite a footpath is signposted to Water End. This leads between fences and via two stiles to a field. Continuing on, the left-hand edge of the field leads to another stile into the corner of a meadow leading down to the River Gade, with the hamlet of Water End across the river above which Gaddesden Place stands majestically. Don't go down to the river (except for a look) but turn right immediately and climb a path up to the trees. Keep straight on along a grassy path near the right-hand edge of the wood and past a hollow in larger trees. Through some pine trees to a junction, by a lot of holly, fork left down to another junction and then right a few metres to a stile. Go straight down across the field to the road at the bottom.

Cross the stile opposite and take a path, a little to the right, to a T-junction at the edge of fields with no boundaries other than differing crops. Turn left and then right along the top edge of the field, below a tall hedge. Across the stile in the corner a path leads ahead, by trees, to another stile and then straight up through trees, by a fence on the left, and then garden fences to the road opposite Potten End Farm. Turn right and follow the main road back to the start in Potten End.

WALK 5
Great Gaddesden - Gaddesden Place
(6km, 3³/₄ miles)

MAPS: O.S. 1:25,000 Pathfinder Sheet 1095
O.S. 1:50,000 Landranger Sheet 166
Chiltern Society Footpath Map No. 20

Climbing eastwards out of the Gade Valley to flatter farm land this attractive short walk passes the Golden Parsonage and Gaddesden Place. Together with Great Gaddesden these two houses are connected with the Halsey family. The rectors of Great Gaddesden were once the Bon Hommes monks of Ashridge but with Henry VIII and the dissolution the church was granted to William Halsey, whose family then remained influential in the area for several generations, as can be seen by the monuments in the church.

Dropping back down there are some fine views of the Gade Valley. The charming River Gade, one of few rivers in the Chilterns, is then crossed at Water End before returning to Great Gaddesden and the start.

START (030,116): On the A4146 from Hemel Hempstead towards

Leighton Buzzard a little past the turning for Great Gaddesden there is some parking by the road opposite a row of pebbledashed houses. Alternative parking can be found in Great Gaddesden.

PUBLIC TRANSPORT: Infrequent buses to Great Gaddesden from Hemel Hempstead.

ROUTE: A footpath to the right of the houses leads by the edge of a field round to the left and then straight up across it into a wood at the top. Immediately fork right at a junction and up a wide path through the trees to a stile into a field. Continue ahead in the field, beside the wood, to a kissing gate and then on to a stile at the end of the next field. Keep straight on, by the fence, past the Georgian front of the much altered The Hoo and to a stile by a gate a little to the left ahead. Follow the hedge on the right and then continue straight across the field to a stile in the hedge opposite and into a large field, aiming for the far right corner. Cross the stiles and farm track to cross the field a little to the left to a stile by an oak, and then on, across the dip of the next field to a stile to a small road.

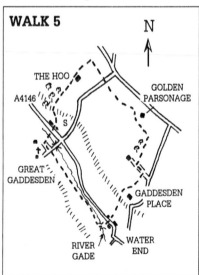

Cross the stile a little to the right on the other side and then cross the large field ahead, past a couple of trees, to a stile beneath a large tree. Go straight on to another stile and then veer left, across a couple more, and past a pond to the drive from the brick and timber Lane House. Turn left and then right along the edge of the field to cross a stile in the corner. Bear left a few metres to another stile into the field facing the Georgian red brick Golden Parsonage with its glorious pedimented doorway. *The Golden Parsonage was the original home of the Halseys since the time of Henry VIII, although the site was obviously occupied long before that. Tumuli have revealed tools of early man and maps shows fish ponds in the grounds. These were an important source of fresh fish in medieval times when religion required the eating of fish on certain days but the sea was too far away. The present building was built in 1705 as the "modern wing" to a sixteenth-century house which was pulled down when the Halseys moved to Gaddesden Place.* Go diagonally right across the corner of the field and to the corner of the next one by a junction of tracks. Take the track, across the one from the house, with a hedge on its left running down into a small valley. Turn right and follow a grand avenue of trees, partly spoilt by horse jumps, and through a gap at the top into the field on the left and along the right-hand edge of this to a farm road.

Turn left a short distance to a stile by a gate on the right and across this. Cross the field towards the corner of trees, whilst to the right is a very Victorian home farm, and on into the next field facing Gaddesden Place to the far right corner and a stile to a track. Go left then veer right to an old gate by a large oak tree. Diagonally to the left leads to one stile and then shortly to another stile overlooking the valley, with the house a little behind to the left. *Built in 1773, for Thomas Halsey, Gaddesden Place is an early example of the architect James Wyatt, who was also responsible for the more exotic Ashridge House nearby. The house had to be rebuilt after a fire in February 1905. During the fire a butler supplying refreshments to the fire fighters was killed when the roof fell in on him.* Descend the field overlooking Water End and the Gade Valley, by the fence on the left, to a stile near the bottom and across the corner of the next field and down to the left of the white cottages to the A4146.

Take care crossing the road at this busy bend and a little to the right a footpath is signposted between buildings and over stiles to a meadow. Drop down, by the fence on the right, to the footbridge over the River Gade. Up to the right-hand corner and cross the stile to the right. Follow the bottom edge of the field and then on, between hedges, to a road opposite The Cock and Bottle in Great Gaddesden. *The church, St John the Baptist, despite the use of bricks from a local Roman villa and its Norman origin has a largely Victorian air, the result of the rebuilding and renovation. Within the church is a chapel and numerous monuments to the Halseys including one to Thomas, Fredrica and their four year old son Ethelbert tragically drowned at sea.* Take the road ahead and, keeping to the right, pass a pump to a stile just before a play area. Go diagonally to the left to the end of the hedge, into the next field and bear right to a footbridge, across the now normally dry river bed, and so up to the stile to the road and the start.

WALK 6
Wendover - The Lee
(12.8km, 8 miles)

MAPS: O.S. 1:25,000 Pathfinder Sheet 1118
O.S. 1:50,000 Landranger Sheet 165
Chiltern Society Footpath Map Nos. 3 and 8

Robert Louis Stephenson, visiting Wendover on his travels, described the town as "a straggling purposeless sort of place" and, 'well down in the midst with mountains and foliage about it'. The first description now seems rather harsh as the town has considerable charm, but, nestling at the base of the Wendover Woods which is the highest point of the Chilterns, the second comment still has a ring of truth. As Wendover Woods is now a blanket of Forestry Commission trees, this walk from Wendover follows the Ridgeway along old lanes, to climb the Chiltern scarp further to the south. On the top, the route visits a cluster of villages around The Lee, passing an ancient church and one of the strangest sights in the Chilterns along the way, as well as enjoying some delightful walking country.

START (869,078): Wendover High Street. There is a car park behind the High Street. Alternative parking on the road by St Mary's Church which is signposted off the A413 Great Missenden road.

PUBLIC TRANSPORT: Wendover is accessible by Chiltern Line trains or by bus.

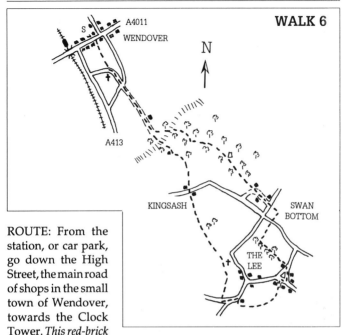

WALK 6

A4011
WENDOVER

N

A413

KINGSASH

SWAN
BOTTOM

THE
LEE

ROUTE: From the station, or car park, go down the High Street, the main road of shops in the small town of Wendover, towards the Clock Tower. *This red-brick edifice, given in 1842 by Abel Smith, is the main focal point of the town and is now a tourist information centre. The lower part of the tower was once used as the town lock-up.* Just before the Clock Tower, turn right onto Heron Path, also signposted as the Ridgeway. Almost immediately the feeling of being in a town is lost as this made path runs at times by the charming stream, which gives Wendover its name, a derivation from the old English for 'a white [chalky] place by a stream'. Across a driveway continue on, to meet a road running past St Mary's Church, which is largely of Victorian appearance but has some fourteenth-century building. *The church was to have been built on a field next to the town but a writer in 1882 describes how the materials were carried away by witches, or fairies, and deposited where the church now stands.*

Turn left along this quiet road to a junction at Wellhead, the source of the stream. At the junction cross the road and go up the farm track signposted as the Ridgeway. Follow this very English track, with the down-to-earth name of Hogtrough Lane, as it climbs between high banks to pass a farm and an avenue of trees leading off to the right. Keep straight on to a Ridgeway signpost at the bottom corner of a wood.

Turn left here and almost immediately left again, so that the conifers are to the right. At a fork turn right (marked as the Ridgeway) and ascend diagonally, through the trees, on a well graded path. Just before the main path levels off a white arrow on a tree marks a small path off to the right. Leave the Ridgeway and climb up this path for fifty metres to a track and turn left. Follow this track, marked by the occasional white arrows, past a new plantation and over a junction to the unusual sight, in the Chilterns, of a trig-point by the side of the track. Surrounded by trees now its line of sight for surveying is rather limited. Keep straight along the track, past a row of beech trees separating it from a field on the left, to a junction with a bridleway. Cross the bridleway and follow the route through an area of replanting, and then on a wide path through an area of beechwoods to an unmade road by gardens and garages. Turn left along the road, past fields and houses, to The Old Swan, a sixteenth-century pub selling good food and beer with a welcoming fire in winter.

Over the road passing Jim's Seat, a small wooden bench, cross the stile and follow the footpath along a grassy strip between wire fences. Continue on to cross a stile and turn right at the junction to drop down via gates to the road. Cross the road and start up the driveway to Kingsvale Farm but then keep straight on, beside a beech hedge to a stile, after the drive swings off to the right. Continue on by the hedge, crossing stiles to the end of the fields, and turning left here along a track in a strip of woods. Keep to the same direction, past a fork-junction in an area of felling, and then along by a hedge in a field to cross a stile and pass through the farm complex to meet the road by Chapel Farm. The gravestones in the front garden give a clue to the naming of the farm and the foundation stone is a reminder of the influence and generosity of the Rothschild family in the area. Cross the road and fork left along the small road into the village of Lee Clump turning right to go past The Bugle pub.

Turn left, down the track signposted as a footpath on the near side of the school, and into the field beyond. Descend to the valley bottom, passing a large pit, to a stile by a power cable post. Cross the stile and go along the green lane, which curves to the right, and across a small road. After a while take care to look for a gap in the holly hedge on the right, opposite a break in the hedge on the other side. This gives access to a path, by the beech hedge boundary of Pipers, to the road.

Just within the entrance to Pipers is one of the most out-of-place sights in the Chilterns, a bow figurehead resembling Admiral Earl Howe, the leader of the Channel Fleet during the French Revolutionary Wars. Now land-locked, this very nautical feature is originally from the last wooden warship to be built for the British Navy, called The Howe and later HMS Impregnable. The reason for its presence in a leafy corner of the Chilterns

Ship's figurehead of Admiral Earl Howe

is due to a local resident, Arthur Liberty, who ran a drapery store in nearby Chesham selling silk from his sister's workshops. When the ship was broken up in the 1920s the timbers were bought by the family and used in the building of Liberty's in Regent Street.

Turn left along the road, in an avenue of oak trees, to the bend, turning off here onto the more minor road, past Hunts Green Cottages. Take the footpath off to the right, along the right-hand side of a field, to a corner of holly hedges and then turn diagonally to the left to cross the field to a stile by a gate. The route continues by the low ridge of an earthwork to a stile but a diversion to the right, across stiles, leads to the two churches of The Lee. *The first encountered is the old church of St John the Baptist which was built in the 1200s, and is a simple buttressed structure of great charm. Past this church is the later Victorian red brick church, provided by the Libertys, which is much less attractive. In the graveyard is a Celtic-style cross commemorating Sir Arthur Liberty.*

Over the stile, cross a track to take the track running along the left-hand side of a field. Past a small wood, continue in the same direction along the edge of fields, ignoring junctions until the corner of a field forces a left turn. Soon a rickety stile in the hedgerow on the right leads to the next field. Follow the right-hand edge of fields, past more junctions, to a gate and concrete track running through a small field. This leads to another track and, a short distance to the left, the road at Kingsash.

Across the road a footpath is signposted to a stile. Follow the side of the field to the trees ahead and then follow the edge of the next field, by the woods, round the corners to the left to a stile by power cable posts. Pass between the white painted house and stables to a stile and footpath between hedges. Entering the woods the path drops straight down, running above a deep cutting for a bridleway near the bottom. At the bottom continue straight on, returning to Hogtrough Lane again and the way back to Wendover.

WALK 7
Ellesborough - Dunsmore
(8.7km, 5¹/₂ miles)

MAPS: O.S. 1:25,000 Pathfinder Sheet 1118
O.S. 1:50,000 Landranger Sheet 165
Chiltern Society Footpath Map No. 3

An attractive climb from Ellesborough, at the base of the Chiltern scarp, below one of the scarp's Beacon Hills, leads to join the Ridgeway at the top as it passes Chequers, the famous country home of Prime Ministers. After visiting the quiet and secluded village of Dunsmore, the walk returns through woods to the scarp at the striking monument on Coombe Hill, the highest viewpoint in the Chilterns.

START (836,067): There is limited parking opposite Ellesborough Church, at the start of a bridleway, on the B4010 Wendover to Princes Risborough road. Alternative parking can be found by heading towards Wendover, on the B4010, and turning right at Butlers Cross towards Great Missenden, parking by the road just past the Bucks Guides Centre joining walk near end.

PUBLIC TRANSPORT: Some buses between Aylesbury and High Wycombe stop at Ellesborough.

ROUTE: Opposite Ellesborough church cross the stile, at the right-hand end of the garden fence, and climb the worn line in the grass through the field towards the right of the dominating Beacon Hill. Over a stile go around the hill overlooking a promontory of trees in which Cymbeline's Castle, a Norman motte and bailey castle, is hidden. *It's often been thought that Kimble is a derivation from Cymbeline and hence Cunobelinus, the King of the Britons who fought the Romans during the first century AD, but it's more likely that Kimble is from the old English for "royal hill" and indeed, in the eighteenth century there was a Belinus's Castle rather than Cymbeline's.* Traversing above the deep

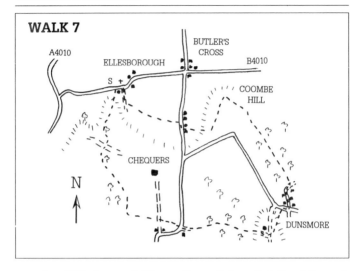

WALK 7

coombe of Ellesborough Warren the path is well defined through elderberry trees and is followed by steps to the top. A signpost at the top indicates the direction, across a field, to trees through which there is a clear path.

Cross the narrow road to a stile by a gate and follow the left-hand edge of the field, with views of Pulpit Hill and the summit of Chequers Knap away to the right. Bend round the trees to the left to the corner of the field and a junction of paths. Joining the Ridgeway path, cross the stile by a white gate and follow the path by the trees along the right-hand side of a field in which Chequers stands backed by Coombe Hill beyond.

Chequers would seem to have acquired its name from Elias Hostiarius, the Usher of the Exchequer between 1170 and 1192, who gained tenure of the estate, and his son Henry de Scaccario (Latin for chequer) who secured the rights and titles to the land. The court of Exchequer derived its name from the chequered table upon which accounts were settled.

Through marriage the estates passed into the Hawtrey family, most notable of whom was William Hawtrey who was responsible for building much of the current house in the 1560s. In 1565 William Hawtrey was also given the task of imprisoning Lady Mary Grey, the youngest sister of Lady

Jane Grey, at Chequers, as she had angered Queen Elizabeth I by marrying in secret, and, despite the difference in rank, Thomas Keys the sergeant-porter. Thomas Keys, by contrast, was kept in Fleet Prison and when he died Lady Mary returned to favour but kept her married name and looked after his children from a previous marriage.

Later the estate passed through various hands, at one time linked to a daughter of Oliver Cromwell and at another time nearly bought by Benjamin Disraeli, until in 1909 Arthur Lee MP became the occupier. He did much restoration work and in 1917 donated Chequers to the nation saying "....the better the health of our rulers, the more sanely they will rule, and the inducement to spend two days a week in the high and pure air of the Chiltern hills and woods will, it is hoped, benefit the nation as well as its chosen leaders." However, Lloyd George the first prime minister to have use of Chequers reported, "It is full of the ghosts of dull people" and that was before all the subsequent politicians!

Continue over the stile bending right to another stile on the left and then drop down through the field to cross Victory Drive, which is lined with beeches donated by Winston Churchill, a little to the left of the gatehouse. Keep straight on, into the field beyond, before bending right past a group of trees to reach the road.

Cross the road and follow the Ridgeway, signposted up the track to the left of the white houses and into a strip of trees between fields. Signs indicate a divergence of the footpath and bridleway but they rejoin fairly shortly, just before a cross-junction of the Ridgeway straight ahead and the South Bucks Way. Follow the Ridgeway up through the beechwoods until it turns left down a ditch and, keeping straight on here, bend right shortly and follow a track past stands of young conifers, birch and old beech trees and down a valley, past other paths, to the bottom at Dunsmore Old Farm.

Over the stile ahead climb diagonally, to the left, out of the valley over a series of stiles to a road and turn right into Dunsmore itself. Just past the village pond turn left along the road signposted "Dunsmore Village only". Beyond The Fox public house this becomes a track with no access for cars and, passing a footpath off to the left, bends right to another junction. Rather than enter the field ahead fork left here over a stile into woods, where the path runs at first between wire fences and then beside old metal railings for quite some distance. Continue past a few junctions with other paths until

Coombe Monument

the metal railings make a distinct turn to the right and keep straight on, along a small path, indicated by white arrows, through once-coppiced beech trees. Turn right along a wider path and then shortly turn left to a stile at the edge of the woods. Passing the National Trust Coombe Hill sign follow the left edge of the open space and then on to the monument.

Built in 1904 (and rebuilt in 1938 after being destroyed by lightning) the monument commemorates the 148 Chiltern men who died during the Boer War and is located at one of the best vantage points on the Chiltern scarp. At 257 metres (832ft) above sea level Coombe Hill is often cited as the highest point of the Chilterns but, in reality, the summit of the Chilterns is hidden in Wendover Woods and Coombe Hill is only the highest open ground of the Chilterns. However the views are still tremendous, stretching across the Vale of Aylesbury as well as along the scarp to Ellesborough Church and Beacon Hill in one direction and to Wendover and the large French-style chateau at Halton in the other.

From the monument follow the edge, seemingly way above a golf course, facing Beacon Hill and Ellesborough Church and, keeping below a narrow strip of bushes and gorse, continue on to meet a stile at a wire fence. Don't cross the stile but turn right and follow the path which drops very steeply through some trees (care is needed when it is wet). At the bottom keep straight on, through a gate, across a path and on to meet the Butlers Cross to Great Missenden road. Turn right, past two houses, to a signpost indicating a footpath across the field to the left. Follow this well trodden path through the dip of the field leading to a track, along which a short distance to the right is the start.

WALK 8
Great Kimble - Whiteleaf Cross
(6.1km, 3³/₄ miles)

MAPS: O.S. 1:25,000 Pathfinder Sheet 1118
O.S. 1:50,000 Landranger Sheet 165
Chiltern Society Footpath Map No. 3

From the village of Great Kimble, at the foot of the Chiltern scarp, this walk climbs the scarp along the North Buckinghamshire Way, to the wooded Pulpit Hill before cutting across to the viewpoint at the top of the cross on Whiteleaf Hill. The return is along a delightful section of the Ridgeway before dropping down to pass through the old settlements at the base of the scarp.

START (826,058): At Great Kimble on the Princes Risborough to Wendover road, just past the church in the direction of Princes Risborough is a small loop providing parking.
Alternative parking can be found at the car park on Whiteleaf Hill, reached from Monks Risborough. Follow the Ridgeway to join the walk at the Cross.

PUBLIC TRANSPORT: Great Kimble is on a bus line between Aylesbury and High Wycombe.

ROUTE: Just prior to the parking loop a well made track signposted as the North Bucks Way climbs from the base of the Chiltern scarp. After a distance the track becomes smaller, although still obvious,

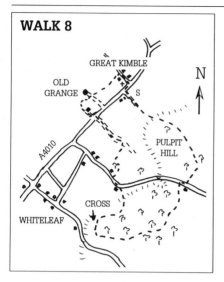

WALK 8

GREAT KIMBLE

OLD GRANGE

S

N

PULPIT HILL

A4010

CROSS

WHITELEAF

and is crossed by the Ridgeway at Chequers Knap. Continuing on there are good views across to Beacon Hill and Coombe Hill Monument as well as across the Vale of Aylesbury. Near the top of Pulpit Hill the path enters a wood, in which are hidden the remains of an Iron Age fort. Keep to the bridleway as it passes a cross junction marked with white arrows and then dips gently, past a break in the trees with views down to Brockwell Farm, before levelling off again. A Y-mark on a tree indicates another junction and cross the stile on the right here to follow the well marked and clear path, descending through the wood, and across a forest track down to a road.

A few metres to the right down the road a bridleway is signposted off to the left, leading round the head of a deep little valley. Continuing straight on at a junction the bridleway now climbs gently among wind damaged beech trees. Blue and white arrows mark the bridleway as it is followed through a right then left junction then, ascending past a forest track, a footpath is marked off to the right a few metres later. Follow this well marked path, which is joined by a bridleway from the left near the top of the wood, to meet the scarp edge in an area of recent clearing. Turn right to follow the Ridgeway footpath along the top to a grassy clearing which marks the top of Whiteleaf Cross.

The origin of Whiteleaf Cross is less than certain. A boundary mark is known to have existed there since AD903, but, despite Massingham's claims that it is a phallic monument of the Late Bronze Age from the evidence of a barrow containing a Neolithic burial chamber on the hill, the

Beacon Hill from Chequers Knap

present form of a cross on a triangular base probably dates from much later. It was possibly cut by medieval monks from Monks Risborough, which it overlooks, although some suggest it was cut as late as the seventeenth century by either side in the Civil War. The triangular shaped base may even be the result of chalk quarrying at the base of the hill which then became adapted and included into the cross. Despite all the speculation as to its origins in 1947 the cross was incorporated into the Buckinghamshire county arms. Little can be seen of the cross from the top due to the slope of the hill and it is best observed from further away in the environs of Princes Risborough. However, the views across the Vale of Aylesbury are as good as anywhere along the scarp.

From the back of the clearing follow the Ridgeway footpath, indicated by yellow arrows and acorns, as it runs along a delightful wooded ridge above a deep wooded bowl called The Hangings. The path drops down the end of the ridge and across a junction to a stile and a track down to The Plough, renowned for its selection of cheeses and as one of the few pubs on the generally abstemious Ridgeway.

Go left to the road and along this for a few metres to a footpath off to the right by a "No Horses" sign. Follow this into a nature reserve turning left, after passing through a gap in the bushes, and on to cross the horse track to find a footpath between two posts with "No Horses" signs in the bushes. This ascends out of the valley near pine trees and along the left-hand edge of a field to its crest. Turn right along the marked Ridgeway across the field which has good views of Pulpit Hill and Chequers Knap. At the other end of the field, after passing through a few bushes, turn left down the bridleway as it descends in a cutting to join a farm road and then on to the main A4010 road.

Cross the road and follow the footpath along the drive to The Grange to a stile at its end, past the house. The right of way in the next field involves walking two sides of a triangle, first across the field to a stile by the corner of a group of trees and then, rather than crossing that stile, turning right and on to a second obvious stile. Don't be tempted to take the short cut as in the trees is the fairly rare (for the Chilterns) sight of a water filled moat protecting the characterful Old Grange, which was originally built in the fifteenth century and belonged to Missenden Abbey. Over the second stile cross the driveway and stile and proceed on towards the village of Great Kimble and its church at the luxuriant base of the Chilterns. At a stile, where arrows mark a junction, take the left-hand, but indistinct, path keeping just to the right of the power pylons across the field which is full of ancient earthworks. Through a stile and gate, to the right of a small lake, a better path leads to a road and turn right, up through the village, to the church of St Nicholas, opposite the Bernard Arms. Turn right down the main road back to the start.

WALK 9
Great Hampden - Little Hampden
(9km, 5½ miles)

MAPS: O.S. 1:25,000 Pathfinder Sheet 1118
O.S. 1:50,000 Landranger Sheet 165
Chiltern Society Footpath Map Nos. 3 and 12

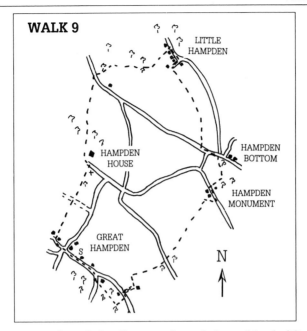

WALK 9

LITTLE
HAMPDEN

HAMPDEN
HOUSE

HAMPDEN
BOTTOM

HAMPDEN
MONUMENT

GREAT
HAMPDEN

N

This attractively varied walk passes through the parkland of Great
Hampden, across the gentle valley to the quiet hamlet of Little
Hampden, down the ridge to Hampden Bottom before climbing
back up to the wooded Hampden Common via the Hampden
Monument.

*As the names suggest the area was historically linked with the
Hampden family. The family were resident here from the Norman Conquest
but it was John Hampden (1594-1643) who brought the name its acclaim
with his role in the events leading to the Civil War. He became a politician,
representing Buckinghamshire and Wendover, and would have emigrated
to America with his then little known cousin Oliver Cromwell to avoid
taxes but for their ship being prevented from sailing. In 1635 Charles I,
despite being at peace, expanded the collection of Ship Money to the inland
counties as a method of increasing taxes. John Hampden refused to pay the
20 shillings he could easily afford and became a test case, which he lost, but
which made him a national figure. In 1640 the House of Commons declared*

the judgement to be "against the laws of the realm". Then, in 1642, John Hampden was one of five MPs the king had impeached on a charge of treason prompting 4000 of his Bucks constituents to ride to London in his support. With the outbreak of the war he was killed in an early action at Chalgrove Field, just north of the Oxfordshire Chilterns, leading a unit to intercept Royalist troops who had sacked Chinnor. His last words were recorded as "O Lord, save my country".

START (845,015): Great Hampden, at the junction of the Speen to Prestwood road and the Bryants Bottom road. This is near the Hampden Arms pub and by the cricket pitch. There is some parking beside the Bryants Bottom road particularly past the cricket pitch by the woods or further on just beyond a right bend (the walk returns along this section of road).

PUBLIC TRANSPORT: There is only an extremely limited bus service to Great Hampden.

ROUTE: Return past the cricket pitch, which plaques inform was created as a war memorial, to the road junction. Follow the small road opposite the Bryants Bottom road bending round to the right. Leave the road and pass between the garage of Martin's Farm and the drive to a part thatched house, on a grassy footpath. This leads between a field and pine wood and then on between open fields. Crossing the farm road at the far end, follow the short track ahead to the kissing gate. From the gate are the first views of Hampden church and behind it Hampden House, set in parkland. The large trees are the remains of old avenues planted to radiate out from the house.

Follow the fence on the left, towards the church, through a couple of kissing gates to pass a tree-enclosed pond to a gate in a picket fence which gives access to the church graveyard. Go round to the left of the tower of St Mary Magdalene Church, a flint perpendicular church (although the door is earlier thirteenth century). *In 1828 the body of John Hampden was exhumed from the graveyard to settle a gruesome argument as to whether he died from gunshot wounds or from the explosion of his own pistol. The discovery of an amputated hand wrapped in a separate cloth favoured the latter cause.*

Go left along the road, past the side of Hampden House which is largely obscured by yew hedges. Just past the recently converted Gothic brick stables on the left the road ends and immediately turn right over a stile. Cross the field in front of the house and a great cedar tree, protected by a ha-ha. *Part of the interior of the house has details from near the time of King John however the outside is pure early Gothic Revival of the early 1750s but is still attractive.*

Enter the conifer plantation via a stile and descend, following the break in the trees, passing a fine redwood specimen to emerge from the woods with views of Hampden Bottom Farm and the gentle valley. Cross the field to the far left corner, following the white marker posts, to a stile and the road running along the valley.

Opposite, a gate leads to a track gently climbing the side of the valley in a narrow band of beech trees. Where the track turns to the left, turn sharply off to the right onto a path that leads in a few metres to a stile and an open field. Bearing slightly right, cross the scoop to a footpath hidden in the hedge running along the top. The path leads through trees to a stile and then, veering slightly left, cross the field and summit of the ridge to a farm track. Go straight on, past a holly tree with a white arrow, and along a path to join the drive to two houses and on to the road at Little Hampden. To the left is The Rising Sun free house with its unusual red and black bricks, a suitable end to the road.

Turn right down the road until it starts to drop and bend to the left, turning right by the grass triangle here go along a small road past a few cottages to a cross-junction of tracks in front of the final house. Turn left on the track that runs beside a field and also shortly a new plantation of mixed trees. At the end of the trees is a good viewpoint looking to the white Court Field House and directly across the valley to Hampden Monument which can just be seen by a bend in a road. Continue downhill on the path keeping to the hedge on the left. Round an S-bend to the end of the field turn left through the hedge, by a power post, and then right along the side of a field by a tall hedge. At the end bend to the right of the pine trees to meet the road near a junction.

Follow the main road to the left, towards Amersham, to a double junction before the red brick thatched Smithy Cottage. Cross the stile on the right, by the signpost to "Little Hampden only", and follow the well marked path, through the trees with bramble under-growth, to join another path and in a few metres further a stile into a field. The field is part of a magnificent avenue with Great Hampden House way to the right and two pepper-pot gate houses to the left. Somewhat before this grand approach was created, Griffith Hampden felt so honoured by a visit of Queen Elizabeth I that he had a section of Grim's Ditch levelled to ease her access. Cross the avenue to a stile and go on, by the edge of woods, to a cross-junction marked with white arrows turning right here to climb in the edge of the trees by a field. Skirt a hollow to the right at the top and, crossing the stile, go on by the fence to two stiles leading to the road where there is a little gate on the left to the Hampden monument.

The sandstone cross nestling below three large sycamore trees is now a little weathered, but the inscription reads "For these lands in Stoke Mandeville John Hampden was assessed in 20 shillings ship money levied by command of the king without authority of law on the 4th of August 1635. By resisting this claim of the king in legal strife he upheld the right of the people under the law and became entitled to grateful remembrance." Overlooking his estate the enclosure enjoys good views across to little Hampden and Cobblershill.

Go left along the road, past Honor House and the footpath signposted at the end of the buildings, to a bridleway and footpath signposted through a small gate to the right beyond a group of trees. Through another gate, at the end of the field, turn left past a pillar with a white arrow and go along by the hedge. Cross the stile and go straight on along the edge of the next field past recent plantation. Dropping into a little valley turn left, into the mature beechwood, and down through holly bushes to a road.

Through a gap in the fence opposite, ascend the marked path keeping near to the right edge of the wood. At the top, exit from the wood and go straight ahead, along the right-hand side of the hedge and around its bulge. Half-way to the next island of trees turn left and go to a stile at the left-hand end of a wooden fence. The path continues between wire fences and across a stile to a T-junction. Turn right, away from the fine Georgian house (the old rectory which was at the end of one of the original avenues of trees from Hampden House) and along the track through large holly bushes to a road by a thatched cottage.

Great Hampden

Turn left along the road for a few metres to the bottom of a gentle dip where a footpath goes to the right by a small tree with a white arrow. Through bushes, trees and bracken ignore a small path to the right but then at a larger cross-junction, which is marked with white arrows albeit badly, turn right beneath cables and climb by an area of bracken. (If a horse track by a deeper valley is reached turn right up this.) The path bends left at the top and, as a horse track converges, keep to the right past a "No Bridleway" sign and through oak trees following the white arrows. Under power cables go through smaller trees to a grassy clearing at the far end of which join a track leading straight on to join the drive from Great Hampden Centre and so on to the road. Turn right up the road for a few metres to a junction and follow the main road round to the left towards Great Hampden and along the edge of the wooded common back towards the cricket pitch and start.

WALK 10
Great Hampden - Lacey Green
(9.3km, 6 miles)

MAPS: O.S. 1:25,000 Pathfinder Sheet 1118
        O.S. 1:50,000 Landranger Sheet 165
        Chiltern Society Footpath Map Nos. 7 and 12

From the Hampden area once much beloved by John Masefield, the poet and once resident of the area, this walk follows the well maintained paths through the Hampden Estate woods. A pleasant little valley then leads to Lacey Green with its historic windmill standing guard at the entrance to the Risborough Gap. Climbing Lily Bottom Lane to the Pink and Lily pub made famous by another poet, Rupert Brooke, the walk returns to Hampden House via a fine section of Grim's Ditch.

START (845,015): Hampden Common cricket pitch near the Hampden Arms public house. There is some parking by the road. It is also possible to start the walk from the northern end of Lacey Green by the windmill.

PUBLIC TRANSPORT: Very limited bus service to Great Hampden, a better option would be to get a bus to Lacey Green from High Wycombe or Aylesbury and start the walk by the windmill and The Whip pub there.

ROUTE: From the Hampden Arms cross the Bryants Bottom road and go along the side of the cricket pitch to a gap and a stile giving access to woodland, dropping away from the plateau of the cricket pitch. Keep on the path marked by white arrows down through the woods, passing a junction off to the left and a large hollow, to reach a road at the base of the valley.
   Turn right up the road to the cross-roads and take the public bridleway by a "give way" sign which leads off into the woods. The Hampden Estate management have to be highly commended for

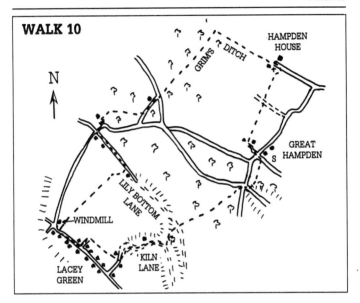

WALK 10

N

HAMPDEN HOUSE

GRIM'S DITCH

GREAT HAMPDEN

LILY BOTTOM LANE

WINDMILL

KILN LANE

LACEY GREEN

their maintenance of this and other public rights of way. Horses and walkers have been segregated, horses confined to a route between wire fences whilst a well marked footpath runs nearby. After a short rise the route levels out for some distance through conifers to cross another path close to the edge of woods. Ahead, pass between wire fences on the bridleway which crosses another track and, as it begins to descend, offers views of Lily Bottom down to the right. For the final drop the bridleway widens as it passes through woodland to the bottom and a junction of valleys and bridleways.

Turn right up the track known as Kiln Lane, which starts to climb this surprisingly deep valley, and where the entrance drive of White House Farm meets this track turn off left up a bridleway climbing steeply between a hedge and the remnants of Grim's Ditch. At the top turn right, and crossing a road, go along a track past the house Datcha to a field. Follow the left-hand side of the field and then, turning left at the end where there are the first views of the windmill, onto a road past houses to the main road running through Lacey Green. Turn right along the pavement to the stile by a bus shelter, shortly before The Whip pub.

The dominating feature of this end of Lacey Green is the windmill. Built in 1650 it is thought to be the oldest surviving smock mill (one where only the top section turns and whose wooden cladding on the sides resembles a smock). Originally situated in Chesham it was dismantled and then rebuilt, with a few modifications, in its present location in 1821 on the orders of the Duke of Buckinghamshire. It was still in operation until 1915 but then, after a short period of use as a weekend cottage, fell into disrepair before regaining a use as a look out post for the Home Guard during the Second World War. It was as late as 1971 before restoration could be undertaken by which time it was a couple of feet out of true. Now maintained by the Chiltern Society, the mill is open for viewing on Sunday afternoons between May and September, and can occasionally be seen in sail.

Across the stile by the bus shelter, go along the hedge to a stile near the cottages and then on to another stile at the end of the hedge. From here continue in the same direction across a series of stiles and fields of this open valley head, dominated by the large farm complex of Widmer Farm away to the left.

Cross the final stile in the series, which is next to a gate, and enter the right-hand option of the two fields ahead. Veering slightly to the right, pass between the hedge and pylon across the field to a stile, and further right cross the corner of the next field to a stile and a bridleway following the remains of Grim's Ditch in a strip of trees. Go left down the bridleway to meet Lily Bottom Lane. Turn left up the road, passing stones marking "35 miles to London" in one direction and "100 thirsty yards" to The Pink and Lily in the other.

The Pink and Lily pub, painted a suitable shade of pink, is 100 yards farther at the junction of Pink Road and Lily Bottom Lane (and also Wardrobes Lane). *The names are derived from a Mr Pink who was once the butler at Hampden House and a Miss Lily, a parlour maid there who married and set up house. The Pink and Lily also has a literary connection for Rupert Brooke, one of the young poets who rose to prominence only to be buried in a foreign field during the First World War, frequented the pub when he was walking in the area with Cathleen Nesbitt. The Pink and Lily's is no doubt among the inn-fires he mentions in his evocative poem "The Chilterns". He also wrote four lines of doggerel about the pub, which are on display inside. The pub has unfortunately been modernised to create more space although there is still one traditional room.*

At the road junction turn right along Pink Road for a few metres before turning off left along a track at the first bend.

By the gates to Hampden Lodge turn right along a bridleway which can be muddy at first. A white arrow on a tree marks a turn to the right before returning to the same direction. Arrows on a tree mark a junction of paths and turn right off the bridleway, past a broken gate, onto a good path through a plantation. Follow this path along to the end through the straight break in the trees and then veer slightly right through a clump of beech trees following the arrows to the road.

Turn left along the road to the junction with the Whiteleaf to Great Hampden road and then follow the footpath signposted in the woods opposite. Initially this path runs along the bank of Grim's Ditch but then, at a marked junction of paths, take the left-hand option to follow the direction of the ditch but a little to the right. The path leaves the wood to continue along its edge in a field across which the tower of Hampden church can be seen. Unsympathetic planting of trees obscures this section of the ditch. Keep to the same direction to enter a plantation at the far side of the field and past a break in the trees to the right to a wooden arch over the path at a junction of ways. Turn right here along another of the excellent segregated bridleways. After a while in conifer trees the footpath crosses the horse track to run along the ruins of the ditch with delightful beech trees. At the end join the track running towards the house and church. Through a gate this passes the Gothic stables and along by a hedge past the house to the church. (See Walk 9 for history.)

At the end of the churchyard leave the road, through a gate to the right, and follow the edge round to the right to the corner of the field and turn left. The path leads to the right of a group of trees and pond, then through a series of kissing gates to one near an old mound. Keep straight on, across a farm road, along a path between two fields and then beside a small conifer plantation to join a road by a thatched cottage. Turn left along the road to return to the start.

WALK 11
Amersham - Great Missenden - Wendover
(18.3km, 11¹/₂ miles)

MAPS: O.S. 1:25,000 Pathfinder Sheets 1138 and 1118
O.S. 1:50,000 Landranger Sheet 165
Chiltern Society Footpath Map Nos. 6, 8, 12, 3.

This walk is exceptional in that it is not a circular walk, but is designed to go between the railway stations of Amersham, Great Missenden and Wendover. The railway follows one of the "gaps" or valleys cutting through the Chilterns and was naturally preceded by an earlier coach route enabling a string of towns to develop. These, Amersham Old Town, Little and Great Missenden, and Wendover all have their own distinctive charm, retaining many of the buildings from the coaching days.

In addition to following the valley past the grandeur of Shardloes and visiting the old towns, the walk climbs to follow the higher ground overlooking the valley. The walk can be split at Great Missenden into two shorter walks of 10.3 and 8kms (6¹/₂ and 5 miles).

START (964,982): Amersham station. There are car parks at the stations as well as in the towns of Amersham Old Town, Great Missenden and Wendover.

PUBLIC TRANSPORT: Metropolitan Tube to Amersham, or Chiltern Line trains between Aylesbury and Marylebone.

ROUTE: From the exit of Amersham station go down to the road junction and turn left under the railway bridge. Cross the road and take the footpath between the railway embankment and Franklin Court. Veering left and up into beechwoods follow the wide path running parallel to a road and keep to the path as it drops through the trees to emerge at the top of a field looking down upon Amersham Old Town nestling in a bowl. Straight ahead a tarmac

WALK 11

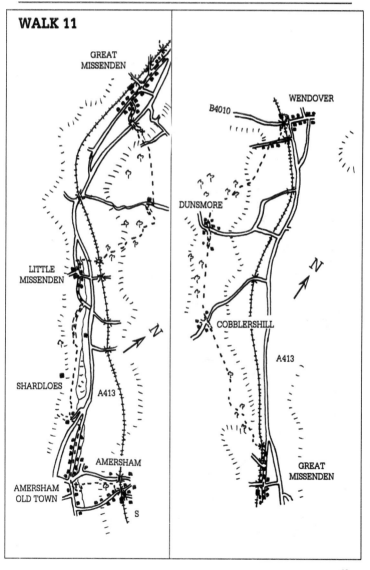

GREAT MISSENDEN

WENDOVER

B4010

DUNSMORE

LITTLE MISSENDEN

COBBLERSHILL

SHARDLOES

A413

A413

AMERSHAM

AMERSHAM OLD TOWN

GREAT MISSENDEN

footpath leads down towards the town, turning left at a junction between cemetery walls and then right over a bridge to the church.

Restored in 1890, the flint Church of St Mary, Amersham has a Victorian appearance on the outside although the majority of the nave dates from the early twelfth century. The attractive inside has several brasses and a very beautiful alabaster monument to Henry Curwen, who came from Workington in Cumberland but died in 1636 whilst in Amersham as a pupil of the rector. Unfortunately the main collection of monuments is in the Drake Chapel which is normally kept locked. The Drakes were a very influential family in the town after 1602 when a marriage was arranged between Francis Drake of Esher and Joan Tothill, the eldest of thirty-three children and heir to nearby Shardloes.

The church may now reflect Christian serenity but it has not always been the case. John Knox denounced Mary Tudor from the pulpit later used by Richard Baxter to argue theology with Anabaptist soldiers of Cromwell's Army. The saddest incidents in Amersham though were the persecution of Lollards, extremist followers of John Wycliffe who criticised the dogmas of the church and the power of priests. An inquisition in 1506 led to William Tylsworth being burnt at the stake, with his daughter forced to light it. However by 1521 the Bishop still considered heresy to be a serious problem in Amersham and so another inquisition ensued and another five men and a woman were burnt on the hill overlooking Amersham.

From the church go left to the main junction in the town and then right past the covered market and along the main road, High Street. *This is possibly the finest town street in the Chilterns lined either side with fine seventeenth- and eighteenth-century buildings. Particularly worth noting are the gifts from two William Drakes; the market hall, with one of its arches enclosed to provide a lock-up, built in 1682 by the nephew of the William Drake (son of Francis and Joan) who had the almshouses built in 1657.*

Keep on out of the town along the left-hand pavement to reach the dual-carriageway bypass and an underpass leading to the gate of Shardloes House. Turn right immediately past the gate house to join the South Bucks Way along a gravel road beside a cricket pitch. From the clubhouse cross the next cricket pitch to the gate with a white notice on it, to the left of the tall trees. The path runs along the bottom of the slope, with trees and a lake to the right, and over a stile with good views of Shardloes above. *The elegant mansion was originally*

The windmill at Lacey Green (walk 10)
Approaching Bradenham (walk 18)

Looking from Puttenham Place towards Penn Bottom (walk 20)
Looking towards Coleshill windmill (walk 21)

designed by Stiff Leadbetter but completed in 1766 by Robert Adam as one of his earliest works. Despite this the Sir William Drake who had it built actually preferred to live in London. The grounds and the damming of the River Misbourne to create the lakes was the work of Humphrey Repton. The house is now divided into private apartments. At the end of the field go a little left to a pair of stiles then along to join a track. Keep straight on along this track crossing another to follow the line of the valley and join a road from the white buildings of Kennel Farm, on the right, and on to meet a road.

Turn left past The Crown free house to the pretty cottages in the village of Little Missenden and the Red Lion pub. Follow the main road, past the junction by the Jacobean Manor House which was once the home of Dr Bates, a member of the Hell Fire Club, to the church.

St John the Baptist, Little Missenden is like a jigsaw puzzle with different parts being built between the Saxon and fifteenth-century periods, but even incorporating Roman bricks. However, most notable in the dark interior are the murals, rediscovered under the whitewash in 1931. The largest of these is the exquisite, thirteenth-century figure of St Christopher carrying the Child Christ over the water. Rather simpler, but even older, is the twelfth-century painted dado.

On the road at the end of the churchyard a footpath crosses over a stile on the right and goes along the right-hand edge of the field to a concrete slab bridge, over the dry grassy riverbed, and on to a stile and the busy A413.

Over the stile opposite go straight up the field with views of the gentle valley. A path leads, via a bridge over the railway, to a junction and turn left into a wood. Climb the good path to the crest where a track crosses from farm buildings on the right. Turn left down the track and out of the wood to cross the dip of a field to the left-hand edge of more trees. Follow the edge of these trees, bending to the right. At the crest of the hill the track bends left to cross an isthmus of fields and follow the edge of more trees bending right. A white painted fence and arrow indicate the path runs in trees next to the edge for the last few metres and then cross the track and stile opposite. Diagonally to the left, between a group of bushes and the corner of a fence, drop down into a steep little valley and turn left along the bottom to a stile and the track again. Turn right up the now concrete track and past stables to a road.

Turn right past the brick, flint and timber Chapel Farm to a footpath, signposted off left just past a gate set in a hedge arch, and bend left through a few bushes and trees to a stile. Turn left along the edge of a field and across one stile straight on to another stile set in a kink of the hedge. Continue along the right-hand edge of the large field and under power cables to the end. Cross the stile and start to descend diagonally to the left, aiming for the gap between woods and a group of trees. Over a small road via stiles start to follow the valley down but then drift to the right and aim for the church which comes into view. A kissing gate leads to the church grounds then go round to the left to reach the main entrance of the church.

The church of St Peter and St Paul, Great Missenden dates largely from the fourteenth-century but has been overwhelmed by nineteenth-century restoration and enlargement including the unusual widening of the tower. Inside several of the early features have been retained along with some brasses and the Aylesbury font.

From the church cross the bridge over the bypass to be rejoined by the South Bucks Way on the road above the grounds of Missenden Abbey. Little remains of the abbey, founded in 1133, and the Gothic house built on the site is now a college. Follow the road left at a junction and past cottages to the main road at the centre of Great Missenden where Amersham and Wendover are both signposted as $4^{1}/_{2}$ miles.

Turn right along the road, whose array of coaching inn and old buildings forms the core of Great Missenden, and keep straight on at a mini roundabout (the station is to the left here). Keep along the Wendover road, past a junction with the Princes Risborough road, and an old toll house. Past Leeward, the last in a group of houses, take the footpath over the stile on the left. Go diagonally right to follow the base of the railway embankment to a tunnel. Through this bend go right across the field to a stile in a nook corner (there is another stile to the field on the left). Slightly left, aiming for the ridge, cross the field to steps up to the next field. Follow the left-hand edge of this field round a group of trees with a view back to the church. Continue along by the edge to a corner and enter the wood along a good path. At the far end of the woods turn right along a

Path down to Amersham Old Town

bridleway between hedges. More open at the top there is a viewpoint across the valley towards Wendover Woods. At the end of the field go straight on, past a junction, into trees and holly. Follow the same direction, never too far from the left edge, to the end where the bridleway continues between hedges. Part way along this a stile on the left can be crossed to continue in the same direction but on the other side of the hedge. This option, which is sometimes less muddy, passes through a couple of fields before rejoining the bridleway as it crosses a track. Continue on to the tiny village of Cobblershill and a road.

Cross the road and follow the South Bucks Way through the gate ahead. Keep straight on along the bridleway, to the left of Colenso (the South Bucks Way forks off left), and continue between fences along the top of the ridge overlooking Little Hampden. Into woods keep straight on along the top near the right-hand edge and on across a break of replanting into beechwoods. At a fork in bridleways keep straight on along the right-hand one and then straight on at a junction of drives, from Hampdenleaf, and along a chipped stone track. Continue past the Black Horse Restaurant to the crossroads by Dunsmore village pond.

Go straight ahead, through Dunsmore Village, to the bridleway past The Fox Inn. Swinging right beside a fence and past a junction off to left the bridleway then diagonally crosses a field between fences to a line of trees. Bend right and descend gently, beside bits of old metal fence on the left, looking for a footpath off to the left which follows the fence descending more steeply. At the bottom bend turn left to climb out of the other side of the valley, following white arrows, and then go round to the right on top. Join a footpath from a stile on the right and turn left (not the faint track ahead) down to a stile and views of Wendover Wood and Halton, a French-style chateau built for Alfred Rothschild but which is now occupied by the RAF. Diagonally left, descend the field to its lowest point then, across a stile, climb diagonally up left between hawthorns and along the edge of a short field to a stile. Straight on, between wire fences then a grassy strip between hedges, leads to a road.

Turn right until just past Newlands where a footpath is signposted to the left across a stile and then diagonally to the right, between pylons, across the field. From this viewpoint of Wendover can be glimpsed the cap, now covered in metal, of the old windmill in the town. A stile leads to a short path between hedges to the road. Turn right over the railway bridge towards Wendover and then left to the station.

WALK 12
Cholesbury - Grim's Ditch
(8.5km, 5¼ miles)

MAPS: O.S. 1:25,000 Pathfinder Sheet 1118
        O.S. 1:50,000 Landranger Sheet 165
        Chiltern Society Footpath Map No. 8

Cholesbury is one of the rural villages on the high ground above Chesham. Like many villages in the area it became involved in the craft of straw plaiting which spread from Luton during the early nineteenth century. Cholesbury even had its own straw plaiters

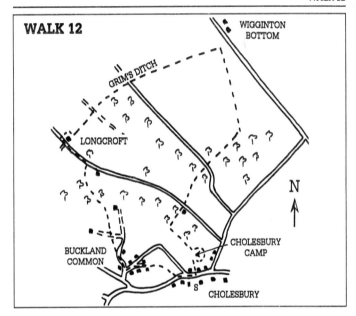

WALK 12

WIGGINTON BOTTOM

GRIM'S DITCH

LONGCROFT

N

BUCKLAND COMMON

CHOLESBURY CAMP

CHOLESBURY

school where children aged four and up were given an education whilst platting, the school fees being paid out of their earnings. As so often in history cheap imports, this time from China in the 1870s, caused the market for local products to collapse.

Keeping to the high ground this relatively level walk passes through the large earthwork of the iron age Cholesbury Camp before following some of the better defined sections of Grim's Ditch.

START (933,071): Cholesbury Common, where there is parking by the side of the road from Chesham. Cholesbury is most easily reached via minor roads from the north end of Chesham, through Hawridge, or from Tring via Wigginton.

PUBLIC TRANSPORT: Bus from Chesham.

ROUTE: The walk begins at the western end of Cholesbury Common past the road off to Wigginton. Follow the footpath signposted to the left of the well-maintained village hall to a stile into Cholesbury Camp which now appears as a large field set in a ring of large beechtrees, broken by the church and a few other buildings to the left. Pre-war excavations revealed evidence of first century Belgaic occupation within the fort.

It is possible to continue straight on across the fort but for a better appreciation of its size turn right immediately within it, alongside a barn, and then continue on to a stile. Cross another stile on the right and climb the earthworks. These largely consist of a deep ditch between mounds of earth, but would once have had wooden palisades as well. Follow the ridge round to the left, although later it may be easier to go along the ditch or outer ridge. After completing a semi-circle the direct path across the fort joins at a gate, at which point turn right and go through the outer ring to a field of scrub and willowherb and on to a stile into woodland.

"Private" notices and a barrier of broken branches ensure the footpath is adhered to through the woods. Over a stile continue straight on along the edge of a field to another stile and woods. Turn right immediately and follow a path amongst beech and silver birch trees parallel to the field to reach the road.

A few metres to the left a signpost, by a stile, marks the way on along the right-hand side of a field by a hedge broken by horse jumping fences. In the woods ahead, cross a wide bridleway and follow the path opposite, past the "please keep to footpath" sign. The path through the mixed woodland is well marked by white arrows and is easy to follow to reach the next road.

Across the road the footpath continues on through a mixture of oak and birch trees, with signs warning this time of traps set for vermin. When the path comes close to the edge of the woods follow the now wider path in the woods parallel to the edge. At the junction of a path joining from the right, and close to where a hedge divides the fields on the left, look for a stile to the left. Cross the field diagonally to the right aiming for the end of a row of hawthorn trees. Grim's Ditch can now be seen ahead and left, marked by a row of trees. Over a stile continue diagonally to the right across the next field towards a stile, however, don't cross this stile but rather go left along by the hedge for a few metres to the line of Grim's Ditch. At this point all that remains is a marginal rise between two fields. Go along this following the obvious path into the trees where the earthworks become much more clearly defined. The path runs parallel to and then along the ridge adjacent to the ditch itself. Although the trees are much more recent than the earthworks they add to the ancient image of the place.

Cross the road and stile and take the right-hand footpath signposted "to Grim's Ditch" at the fork. Follow the path, ascending through the woods by the remnants of the ditch. Leaving the woods, continue straight on across a field where the ditch has been obliterated, although a row of trees ahead suggest its continued line. Crossing a farm track take care to find the path in the centre of this strip of trees. Under the protective cover of the trees the ditch does re-emerge but never as well formed as before. Go to the right, out of the end of the woods, and then turn left by the edge of a field to reach a road.

Turn left along the road, past Longcroft, and on to reach a footpath signposted across a stile into a field with two barns opposite a wood. A gentle climb through the field leads to a stile, by a white gate, and a footpath in mixed woodland with a lot of birch and evergreen shrubs. At a junction keep straight on along the path marked 25A. Keep to the same direction until shortly after an unmapped path joins from the right, the path bends sharply to the left. Turn off right here onto a less obvious path that soon leads to a stile into fields. (If the junction is missed follow the main path to meet a track at the end of the wood and turn right down this, which becomes a road to Buckland Common green.)

Follow the fence along the left-hand side of the field, across a dip, and then round by the side of a broken hedge to a stile. A few metres ahead, in the next field, cross the stile in the hedge on the left and go through the gap to the right into another field. Go along by the hedge on the left to a stile and track across which a gap gives access to another field which is crossed to reach a stile by a gate.

Turn right along the road, dropping past the green of the rather scattered village of Buckland Common. At the road junction turn left up Parrots Lane, passing some thatched cottages, and then turn right at the junction by Stone Cottage. At the end of the road a signpost indicates that the public footpath continues through the gate to the Potteries and on to a stile by a wooden garage. Keep to the right in the field ahead to a stile and then slightly to the right to a gate in the middle of a field and straight on to reach the road. Turn left up the road which in a short distance leads back to Cholesbury.

WALK 13
Hawridge
(9.5km, 6 miles)

Maps: O.S. 1:25,000 Pathfinder Sheet 1118
        O.S. 1:50,000 Landranger Sheet 165
        Chiltern Society Footpath Map Nos. 8 and 17

After a visit to Tring Grange Farm, which is tucked away in its own little valley, this route climbs through the common to the crest of Hawridge. Passing Hawridge village and the remains of a ancient encampment the walk has an open and airy feel, with no valleys but only other ridges visible. The walk returns by one of these invisible valleys which, in reality, is only a couple of hundred metres away from the ridge but by contrast is much more intimate.

START (935,070): The junction of the road from Cholesbury to Chesham via Hawridge, and the Bellingdon road near the Full Moon pub. There is plenty of parking on the common opposite the junction.

PUBLIC TRANSPORT: Buses from Chesham to Cholesbury.

ROUTE: On the common at the start a small stone obelisk marks the boundary between Cholesbury and Hawridge. Follow the treeline, to the left, along the common to the edge of the cricket pitch. The stocks adjacent to the pavilion are presumably for the punishment of batsmen scoring ducks. A stick-man symbol on a post marks a footpath veering off into the trees on the right. This path is only one of a number of paths and bridleways criss-crossing in close proximity, however keep descending to reach the bridleway running along the

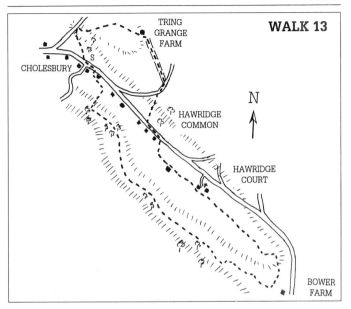

bottom of the valley close to where it meets the road at Cholesbury Bottom.

Turn right along this bridleway for a short distance, but just before it bends to the right round some trees look for a stile into the field on the left. Climb up, through the field, to a stile by a gate and then straight on to another stile over a double fence. Glancing back to the start and Hawridge all that can be seen is the windmill towering above the trees. Go along the right-hand fence to a stile and a track leading down to the white painted Tring Grange Farm and, passing the house and stables, turn right to follow the farm road down the gentle valley. At the junction with the public road turn right along the road and as starting to climb, passing a bridleway off to the right, look for a small path leading off to the left. This path soon begins to climb more directly, initially beside a row of hawthorn bushes and then crossing a couple of paths to meet the Hawridge road. (Again there are many paths on this section of the common and any that climbs to the Hawridge road will do.)

Turn left along the common by the road, passing the working blacksmith, to a stile on the right just beyond the house Field View. Cross the field, diagonally to the left, to the stile at the junction of a hedge and a fence. Over the stile follow the fence to its end and another stile. A narrow path then leads along by the hedge in front of Hawridge Place crossing, first the drive to the house and then at the end of the hedge Hawridge Lane. *Now little more than a narrow bridleway between banks Hawridge Lane was once the main road through Hawridge. The road to Cholesbury and Chesham is a relatively recent construction, a seventeenth-century map would show Hawridge Lane connecting the village to Bellingdon and roads in the other direction to Wigginton and Berkhamsted. Cholesbury and Hawridge villages were more concentrated around their respective centres, rather than the present ribbon development connecting the two, and Hawridge probably had closer ties to Berkhamsted than Chesham.* In the large field beyond Hawridge lane keep to the same direction, following a line of power cable posts and then on beside a hedge. Continue along the edge of the next field, behind a large barn conversion, to a flint barn.

At the far end of the barn a short diversion to the left over a stile leads to the old heart of Hawridge. *St Mary's Church, largely constructed of flint with a wooden bell tower, was built in 1856 replacing an older church which had fallen into disrepair. The carved lead font in the church is a relic from the earlier building. To the right is Hawridge Court, a part timbered house, set into the remains of old earthworks. Fifteen feet high and fifty feet across the earthworks are probably the remains of a Belgaic camp and possibly an outlier to the large fort at Cholesbury (see Walk 12). Hawridge Court was also the site of one of the few deep wells on the ridge, the rest of the village, as elsewhere in the Chilterns, having to rely on collection tanks and ponds filled with rain during the winter months to last out the summer. Piped water only reached the village in 1935, whilst drainage was installed as late as 1963.*

Back at the barn go along beside the earthwork to a stile and on to another stile in the corner of the next field. The path now follows the crest of the ridge on a grassy strip between fields, with views across to the house Thorne Barton. Keep on to the end of the second pair of fields and, passing through the gap in the hedge, turn left and then right to follow the edge of the next field. This field starts to drop steeply off the end of the ridge with views towards Chesham. At the bottom of the field go left to the stile and then down and back, over the broken gate, into the field below. Descend by the edge of the field to the valley bottom and through the gates in a double fence climb to a bridleway running below a hedge.

Turn right along the bridleway away from Bower Farm and, beyond a footpath signposted off to the left, swing up left along below the trees. Keep on along the bridleway, which enters the woods, until it bends left and starts to climb. Turn right here, to cross a stile, and then go left along the valley bottom. Turning right and then left at the end of the first field keep to the bottom of this gentle valley for quite some distance. Often beside trees the valley seems very remote from the ridge but in reality is only a a few metres away. Crossing the track of Hawridge Lane gives one of the few indications of relative positions on the ridge. Continue along the valley bottom crossing stiles and into a woods, consisting mostly of young ash trees, and then past an old gate into older trees. Ignore a footpath off to the right to proceed past a wooden gate, along the valley bottom on a path through the bushes below power cables. At a stile a junction is marked by arrows; and turn right here to climb by the side of fields to the top of the ridge once again. At the corner of the field turn left, towards the windmill, crossing a stile along to the stile in the holly hedge on the right. *The windmill, which was working until the First World War, is a brick tower mill built in 1884 upon the site of an earlier smock mill but using the existing fantail and machinery. The mill is now a private residence.* Cross the stile towards the road and then go left between a wire fence and a hedge, which leads to the road by The Full Moon public house. Originally, presumably before inflation, the pub was called The Half Moon. The start is almost opposite.

WALK 14
Chipperfield - Sarratt
(9.5km, 6 miles)

MAPS: O.S. 1:25,000 Pathfinder Sheets 1119 and 1139
O.S. 1:50,000 Landranger Sheet 166
Chiltern Society Footpath Map No. 5

Chipperfield is barely much more than a hamlet of flint cottages, inn, old school and church, clinging to the corner of a large wooded common. According to a local in 1902 "the common is just the place for a walk before breakfast with a weighted stick when you're getting in condition". Although I advise leaving the stick and having breakfast first, the start and end of this walk does cross different areas of the common making it ideal for those getting "in condition".

Passing the elevated Kings Langley Lodge the walk then crosses a series of pleasant ridges and valleys to the village of Sarratt. This attractive village, astride a long narrow green, was once the home of several stars of the Elstree film studios. The walk then soon returns to woods of Chipperfield Common.

START (044,017): The crossroads in Chipperfield by the Two Brewers Inn. There are a number of car parks along the edge of the common opposite.

PUBLIC TRANSPORT: Limited bus service to Chipperfield.

ROUTE: *The Two Brewers Inn, at the edge of the common, originally dates back to sixteenth century although even up to sixty years ago only occupied the middle of its present building. Rooms at the back of the inn were once used for training well known prize-fighters, hence the quote of 1902.* Head away from the Two Brewers Inn, along the common parallel to the Bucks Hill road and past the edge of car parks, to enter the woods on a large path marked as a heritage trail. Keep to the main path, marked with green outline arrows, through the varied trees, many

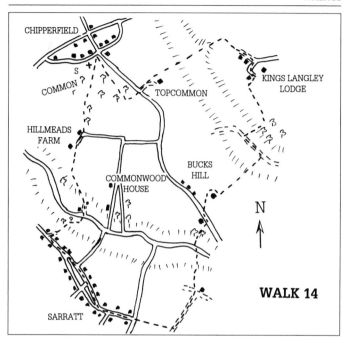

CHIPPERFIELD

COMMON S

TOPCOMMON

KINGS LANGLEY LODGE

HILLMEADS FARM

BUCKS HILL

COMMONWOOD HOUSE

N

WALK 14

SARRATT

of which are large, and past a couple of mounds to reach Apostles Pond, so named because of the twelve lime trees that once circled it. These trees are now heavily pollarded and less than twelve in number, with Judas Iscariot no doubt being the first to go, and so replacement trees were planted in 1984 for the future.

Fork left by the pond for a few metres to a junction of two large paths and bisect these on a minor path through brambles and tall holly bushes (if a "turn around" sign is reached the junction has been missed). Follow this path straight on for some distance to cross a horse track and then to reach the road near a pond.

Across the road, go along the drive of Topcommon to a stile, on the left, and then continue in the same direction over a series of stiles passing below the stables and hen coops. Follow the left-hand edge of the fields beyond, descending to the bottom of a valley across which Langley Lodge Farm can be seen. Pass through bushes at the

Kings Langley Lodge

bottom to climb up ahead on a footpath between wire fences along a shallow side valley. At the top of the field the path staggers a few metres to the left and is then later joined by another path from the left. Keep straight on by the hedge to a stile where a footpath is signposted to the right up a track. This track soon leads past barns and houses, becoming a farm road with views back left to Kings Langley and ahead left to Abbots Langley.

Turn right at the road junction, passing the asymmetrical fronted Georgian house, and round to the left between two ponds. Across the larger pond to the left is the pleasant Victorian brick Kings Langley Lodge. *Kings Langley, as the name suggests, was once the site of a royal palace, which was built by Henry III but no longer exists. The palace was used by several kings including Richard III who was jeered at by women whilst riding through Chipperfield. Showing little tolerance for the voice of his subjects, the king then made a decree that all widows of the parish would not be allowed the dowries from their husbands estates when the men died intestate.*

Turn right, between the farm sheds and a house, to a stile and then onto a wide track between wire fences. Before the track starts to drop turn left over a stile by a signpost. Cross the field to a broken stile and then go diagonally to the right to a stile by a metal gate, with good views across the valley on the right. Continue on by the fence towards the woods ahead and a stile in the corner of the field. Turn right along the edge of the woods, dropping into a deep little valley.

Go down to the bottom and turn left along the track following the secluded valley. At a junction, beyond the end of the woods on the left, turn right up a track climbing directly through a field to run beside the right-hand side of a plantation at the top. Keep straight on at a junction of tracks and go along the left-hand side of fields towards a farm. Turn right and then left, by a fence, round buildings to a stile and then across the field-cum-garden to the stile in the far left corner to gain access to the road.

Turn left a few metres along the road, past Buckshill Cottage, to a footpath signposted to the right between a shed and the fence of a field. This path soon leads right then left round the car park of the cottage, and into the holly bushes and trees. A traceable path meanders avoiding obstacles through the woods down to a road at the bottom.

A few metres to the left, along the road, take the footpath signposted straight up the field opposite and keeping to the right of a tree screen at the top. Continue onto a track past farm sheds to a concrete road and then, almost opposite, along a wide track between hedges. Follow this, until beneath the electricity cables, and turn right through a gap in the hedge and along by a row of posts to a stile and the roads at the edge of Sarratt.

Follow Dimmocks Lane, signposted toward Chipperfield, shortly to reach Sarratt village green. Past the dried out pond, The Cricketers pub, and the wet pond the long green has a road and a straggle of houses either side. Climbing over the crest keep on past The Boot, with its ancient trees supported by struts, and the unusual drum water pump, which has lain idle since the 1920s. Continue on after the roads have rejoined going past The Old Wheatsheaf, now a house, and past another muddy pond in a dip to where a footpath is signposted to the right along a track opposite the start of a flint wall. Go along this track, past the drives to houses on the right, and then along a short grassy track to a stile into the right-hand field ahead. Following the left-hand edge of the field down into a valley the black and white end of Commonwood House can be seen on the other side. *Described by Massingham as "seven Moreton Old Halls, as reconstructed at Hollywood, transhipped in segments, touched up in the Tottenham Court Road and then set in a row on Commonwood Common" it is well worth driving past en route home.*

Cross the stile at the bottom and go right for a few metres along the road before turning left up the track past Dellfield House to a stile at the end of the yew hedge. Climb up diagonally across the field, aiming for the solitary trees to the right of the wood at the top, to reach a stile in the corner of the field. Follow the right-hand edge of the field beyond, bending round to the right to a stile by a gate at the attractive Hillmeads Farm. Go ahead to a stile, to the left of a black wooden stable, and then turn right along the farm road. At the corner, past Hillmeads Farm Cottage, continue straight on along a footpath between a hedge and trees. This path enters Chipperfield Common at a stile by a gate. Cross the main bridleway and go straight on, along a footpath past a "no horse riding" sign. Keeping straight on a clear path leads through the trees, and with a short right and left turn at the end onto the green near the cricket pavilion. Past the church is the Two Brewers and the start.

WALK 15
Chenies - Latimer
(9.2km, 5³/₄ miles)

MAPS: O.S. 1:25,000 Pathfinder Sheets 1138 and 1139
O.S. 1:50,000 Landranger Sheets 165 and 166
Chiltern Society Footpath Map No. 5

The Chess Valley, running between Chesham and the River Colne, is undoubtedly one of the gems of the Chilterns. It is a little unusual for the area in having an idyllic stream of crystal clear water along its length. The Chess Valley Walk, a waymarked linear path, now follows the valley but this walk, in addition to exploring the best part of the valley, also climbs the sides to the attractive old church

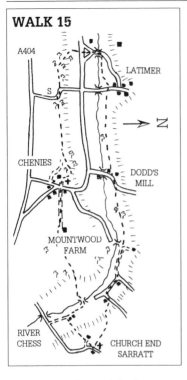

WALK 15

A404

LATIMER

S

N →

CHENIES

DODD'S MILL

MOUNTWOOD FARM

RIVER CHESS

CHURCH END SARRATT

at Sarratt and to Chenies which is steeped in charm and history.

START (006,982): Turn off the A404 at the eastern edge of Little Chalfont onto Stony Lane signposted to Latimer and Flaunden. There is parking on the left by the large bend. Although it is possible to park by the green at Chenies this unnecessarily spoils the village.

PUBLIC TRANSPORT: There are buses to Chenies from Watford and Amersham, except for Sundays.

ROUTE: A few metres down the road a bridleway is signposted off to the left of a forestry road and then runs near the top edge of the wood. Shortly before the bridleway exits the wood turn right, between posts, and descend the wide path down through the trees to a stile at the bottom. Follow the edge of the field to the road, looking across to the imposing red brick Latimer House. *This Victorian house includes a drawing-room from the earlier house on the site to which Charles I was brought as a prisoner in 1647.*

Through the gate across the road, cross the field to the far corner and another gate. Latimer Park Farm, to the left, is the site of a Roman villa. Cross the bridges ahead over the River Chess and then turn right, over a stile, to follow the fence above the long narrow fishing lake. Near the footbridge over the lake, veer left through a group of trees and continue to a stile by some road signs.

A little diversion, up the road to the left, leads to the delightful Latimer village green. On the green is the tomb of a horse brought to England by Major General Lord Chesham in 1900 after it had been wounded and its rider, General de Villebois Mareuil, killed at the battle of Boshof in South Africa.

Over the road, the Chess Valley Walk is signposted over one stile and across a small gravelled area to another. On past an isolated tree, a thin worn path emerges to follow the line of the valley to a stile by a gate. *Along by the fence there is the tomb of William Liberty (died 1777) beneath two oak trees. Related to the famous store family, he was a brick maker who desired to be buried here on his estate (although a little way back in the bushes by the river is hidden the remains of a church, St Mary Magdelena, also associated with the family). The tomb is all that remains from his manor on the hill above.* Continue on to a junction, and through the gate ahead, follow the bridleway. The route is soon joined by the river flowing towards the farm at Chenies Bottom and Dodd's Mill, which until 1933 was still used for grinding corn. Pass between the farm sheds and house hedge to a road by a farm shop.

Turn left along the road and cross a stile at a bend by an oak tree to go along above a bank to a second stile and a path to another shortly in a hedge. Continue to a stile in the far corner and a path leading through trees and bushes. Go straight on across the field to a stile and then slightly right through three oak trees to a stile and road at a bend by a footbridge across the river.

Follow the concrete road, in the direction of the valley past watercress beds, to a junction by a white cottage. Turn right and then, at the next junction (with a cul-de-sac), left up past Cakebread Cottage. Just past the drive, a footpath is signposted to Church End through a gate into the field on the right. Climb the right-hand side of this field to cross a stile into the next field. Turn left to follow round the top edge of this field whilst overlooking the Chess Valley. At the far corner a track leads on between trees to a stile into the field at the top. Keep on by the holly hedge to the corner and a stile leading into the churchyard.

The church of Holy Cross, Sarratt, is a typically delightful Chiltern church and was once the centre of the village which later moved some distance to the north leaving the church, The Cock pub, a row of almshouses and the large house Goldingtons in isolation. Overlooking the Chess Valley the site's religious connections date back to the Roman times from when burial vases have been found suggesting it was a cemetery. The outside of the present church is a jumble of flint walls and tile roofs given a curious air by the saddleback roof (at right-angles to the nave) on the fifteenth-century tower. The core of the church was built when the village belonged to St Albans monastery (about AD1190) in the shape of a cross, and later added to until the current shape dating from 1864-6 when Sir George Gilbert Scott, the famous architect who had worshipped here as a boy, undertook a major restoration and extension including underpinning the existing walls which had no foundations.

Inside the church seems even smaller and more haphazard. Amongst the many features are the fourteenth-century murals and a Jacobean pulpit, the consequence of a decree by James I in 1604 that every parish church should possess a pulpit.

Leave the churchyard and cross the stile between two gates to the right of the almshouses, which were originally built by Baldwins in 1550 but then later rebuilt by Ralph Day in 1821. A footpath leads to cross the drive to the house and, over a stile, into a field to drop straight down the side of the valley beside a iron fence.

Cross the stile at the bottom and go down to the T-junction below the cottages, turning right to another stile. Follow the line of the valley along the field which still shows the terraced remains of strip lynchets created by medieval farmers. At the end, turn left and cross the stile and footbridge over the river. Then continue straight on, through the water meadow and passing a junction, to reach a stile into the trees ahead. Over the stile, immediately turn right to cross a second stile and then go left into a field. Climb the field ahead, to the far hedge and go to the left beside this to the far corner. Turn right and along the edge of next field to a stile in the corner and a track leading to a path between fences around to the left of the sheds of Mountwood Farm. Join the long straight drive which leads to Chenies village. Over the green a gravel road leads past the church to Chenies Manor.

Chenies derives its name from the Cheyne family who acquired the estate around 1200 before which it was called Isenhampstead. After several generations it was inherited by Anne Sapcoate, who married John Russell from Dorset. A member of a family of wine importers, John Russell's knowledge of Spanish proved useful when Archduke Philip, en route to claim the kingdom of Castile, was forced by storms to shelter in Weymouth. This lead to John Russell's introduction into the court of Henry VII and later to become a trusted diplomat for Henry VIII, who visited and even held court at Chenies. Granted the title of Earl of Bedford on Henry VIII's death John Russell had also been given large estates in Tavistock, Cambridgeshire, Woburn and Covent Garden by the king partly as a result of the dissolution of the monasteries. These with later acquisitions such as Bloomsbury in London formed the basis of the family's great wealth. Chenies remained the Russell's main home until after the Civil War, during which a skirmish there resulted in the death of John Hampden's son. Even after they had moved to Woburn, though, Chenies remained in the Russell family until sold to the present owners in 1954 to pay for death duties.

The house is a bit of a jigsaw puzzle with a crypt from a thirteenth century house under the centre of the present house. This was built about 1460 by the Cheynes and then greatly enlarged between 1523 and 1526 by Russell, who also added the distinctive tall chimneys. Only part of the finished warm brick Tudor mansion remains but it still retains great charm. The house and gardens are open Wednesday and Thursday afternoons in summer.

St Michael's Church also reflects the wealth of the house's owners. Completely rebuilt in the fifteenth century and reworked in the nineteenth century the outward appearance has little of distinction, however, inside is another matter. In the main body of the church are a collection of brasses from the Cheyne period, whilst to the side is the Bedford Chapel built in 1556 after the death of the first earl and now according to Pevsner "the richest single storehouse of funeral monuments in any parish church in England". A plethora of marble monuments and altar tombs commemorate the Russell family who have provided the country with soldiers, sailors and statesmen including a Prime Minister. Unfortunately the chapel is kept locked but can seen through the windows which separate it from the church.

Turn right at the gate to the house, onto a path between brick walls leading down to a wood. Fork left, to traverse high in the wood, keeping straight on as other paths join, to a stile at the end and a particularly good viewpoint overlooking the valley and Latimer. Follow the track ahead and through trees at the end to the road by the car park.

WALK 16
Bledlow - Radnage
(12.1km, 7¹/₂ miles)

MAPS: O.S. 1:25,000 Pathfinder Sheets 1117 (for very short
section only) and 1137
O.S. 1:50,000 Landranger Sheet 165
Chiltern Society Footpath Map Nos. 7 and 14

The name Bledlow is possibly derived from the Anglo-Saxon for
Bloody Hill relating to a battle between the Danes and Saxons that
took place here. Now, however, it is a delightful village complete
with an eighteenth-century manor house and Norman church
nestling at the bottom of the Chiltern scarp. Over the scarp the walk
drops to the medieval Radnage church, once the centre of a village
which has now dispersed into several satellite hamlets. The route
then crosses Bledlow Ridge to climb the isolated Lodge Hill on the
return to Bledlow. Although the walk involves more ascent and
descent than normal it is more than worth it for the views.

START (776,020): Bledlow by The Lions pub. This is most easily
reached from the B4009 Chinnor to Aylesbury road turning off
along West Lane to Bledlow. There is some parking on the road by
the grass triangle or further along towards the village and church.

PUBLIC TRANSPORT: A limited bus service from High Wycombe
goes to Chinnor via Bledlow Ridge (not Sundays). Join the walk
near the Boot pub.

ROUTE: From the right-hand end of The Lions, a seventeenth-
century inn which was originally three shepherd's cottages, go
through the wide gap in the hedge on the right and follow the
signposted footpath diagonally across the field past the wooden
power cable post. Join a bridleway at the far corner of the field and
follow this track to the right which gradually steepens towards
Hempden Wainhill at the foot of Wain Hill which is covered by the

trees of Bledlow Great Wood.

Through the gate in front of the house go round the right-hand side of the house and to the left of the gate to Wainhill Cottage. Then immediately fork left on a bridleway signposted between a yew hedge and wooden fence. The bridleway climbs up the hill in a considerable trench, although a path also runs along the top of the right bank. Part way along, and easily missed, a clearing can just be made out through the trees on the left. *This is the site of Bledlow Cross, a simple small cross cut into the chalk, who's origin remains a mystery. Although some writers suggest the cross is contemporary with the Icknield Way, it could easily have been created as late as the early seventeenth century. To reach the cross itself requires scrambling up a precipitous little path through the trees at the far end of the clearing.*

The paths of the ditch and bank join and then follow the left-hand edge of a small clearing to the top. The bridleway is rather churned up here and can be avoided by following a path to the right past posts and through bushes to run beside a wire fence in another clearing. Follow this, looking down upon Chinnor, the scene of much action during the Civil War, go to the far end and then take the path diagonally to the left through the trees to rejoin the bridleway. This meets a narrow road where, turning left then right, go past the flint Hill Top Cottage and along the quiet lane.

Turn left, along the road to the entrance to Woodlands Farm on the left where a footpath is signposted through the hedge. Cross a small field to a stile in a gate and then continue on across another small field to another gate. Go on between sheds and along a track between fields with peasant views across the top of a valley. A stile at the end leads back to the road; turn right to the sharp bend.

At the corner take the footpath across the stile to the left and along the left-hand side of the field. At the far end of the field over the stile a track traverses straight on along the top of beechwoods to the next field. Follow the left-hand edge of this field, by the hedge which runs along a narrow spur, dropping steeply to a stile at the bottom. Cross this quiet little valley enclosed by the steep side of Bledlow Ridge on the left, aiming for the gate near the far left corner. Join the bridleway leading on between hedgerows and keep straight on as it joins a metalled road from Daws Hill Farm on the left, climbing at the end to reach the main road. Turn left downhill past

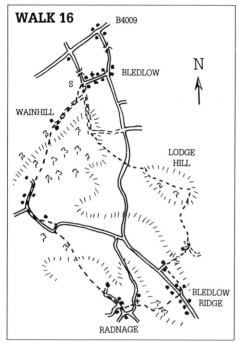

WALK 16
B4009
BLEDLOW
S
WAINHILL
N
LODGE
HILL
BLEDLOW
RIDGE
RADNAGE

a cottage complete with a well in its garden to a footpath sign at the end of its wall. Cross the drive and over a stile into a field then head towards the church. Over the stile at the far end, follow the drive up to the church.

St Mary the Virgin, Radnage, is one of those delightful Chiltern churches that seem to encapsulate history. Built on the foundations of one or two earlier churches it's been a site of worship for a considerable time, probably since Saxon times when landowners raised churches on their lands in order for them to be classified as manorial and entitle themselves to privileges. The font in the church was dug up in a nearby field and is possibly of Saxon age. With a nave that was altered more than once and a splendid roof and tower dating from a transitional style between Norman and early English the structure is much as it would have been in the fifteenth century. Inside is decorated with murals most noticeable of which are various texts. These date from the Georgian period but in places have been covered by coarser Victorian script. Lost beneath white-wash until recently some earlier thirteenth-century murals have also been uncovered. These include the tree of life above the tower arch and fragments of a picture of St Christopher on the north wall.

From the church porch, go the length of the graveyard to steps in the flint wall. Go diagonally to the right across the field to a stile and then slightly left to the top corner of the next field and a stile into the edge of a wood. Climb a few metres up the edge and then before a stile on the left, turn right onto a small footpath leading gently uphill through the trees. At an opening climb directly up by the side of the trees on the left to the top where the path re-forms, leading into an area of hawthorns and elderberries. Emerging from the woods the path goes along by a fence with a dramatic view down to the valley on the right, seemingly way below although actually close by. Crossing a stile the path approaches the back of the houses of Bledlow Ridge and the road that runs along the crest of the ridge.

Cross the road (along which to the left is The Boot pub) and follow the track past the Cherry Tree Cottage. Where the track ends at Crendon House take the path on the left between a fence and the hedge to its end. Cross the stile to the left of the gate and follow the level path with views to Lodge Hill and across the wide valley to Lacey Green windmill (see Walk 10). *Bledlow Ridge once had its own post windmill but by the 1930s this had become very derelict and has now gone.* Over the stile continue on by the fence to meet a small road. Turn right to the end of this and cross the stile beside a gate ahead. Descend the ridge, bearing a little to the left to a stile at the bottom left corner. Over the stile turn left, towards the farm buildings, and then right along the farm road and away from the farm to a right-angled bend. Turn left onto a pebble track, and leaving this where it turns left towards a barn conversion to continue along the bridleway. Keep by the hedge on the left as the bridleway heads towards the attractive valley between Bledlow Ridge and Lodge Hill.

At the end of the field turn right and past a junction to ascend the side of the ridge along the edge of the field. Passing through a gap at the top traverse below the young hawthorn bushes round to the eastern side of the hill. Through a gap in the overgrown hedge turn left at a faint T-junction and climb steeply uphill on a footpath. Crossing the stile painted with a white acorn for the Ridgeway concrete markers indicate the obvious grassy path through the clusters of shrubs and brambles. Passing through a row of beech trees the path continues along the crest of an open narrow ridge with good views towards Whiteleaf Cross (see Walk 8). Descend the end of the hill on the obvious path through denser shrubs and along the edge of a field to a stile into the field on the left. Cross the field, and a bridleway, to a stile and then straight on across the corner of the next field to a stile and road.

Across and to the left a stile with an acorn leads to another gentle climb by the side of a field. At two stiles in rapid succession on the left take the second and keep to the hedge on the right down a dip before climbing up to a stile just below the trees of Wain Hill and turn left onto the Icknield Way (and the Ridgeway). After a few metres turn right below the power cables and follow the bridleway straight on down between the trees and bushes draped with clematis, all the way to The Lions.

WALK 17
Bradenham - Lacey Green
(10.8km, 6³/₄ miles)

MAPS: O.S. 1:25,000 Pathfinder Sheet 1138
O.S. 1:50,000 Landranger Sheet 165
Chiltern Society Footpath Map No. 7 and 12

This walk circles, to the east and north, from the delightful village of Bradenham to Lacey Green. Through a varied landscape of beech woods valleys and ridges the route passes some of the most evocatively named places in the Chilterns, including Flowers Bottom, Turnip End, and just for good measure the Promised Land.

START (828,971): Bradenham village green just off the A4010 High Wycombe to Princes Risborough road. There is a car park at the top right corner of the green reached by a small road from the bottom end and along the right-hand edge of the green.

PUBLIC TRANSPORT: Bradenham is on a number of bus routes from High Wycombe and Aylesbury.

ROUTE: *Bradenham retains the essential English charm of many of the*

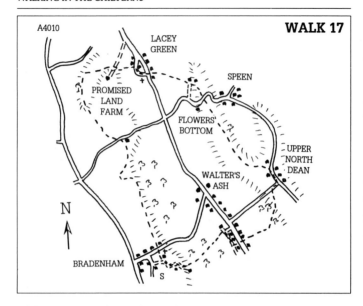

Chiltern villages, clustered around a green with a cricket pitch in front of a church and Georgian manor house. The manor house with its simple geometrical lines softened by the warm red bricks is dated by Pevsner as 1670, but its fame lies in its occupants rather than its architecture. In 1829 Isaac Disraeli, the author of Curiosities of Literature, *came to live here with his 13-year old son Benjamin. Avoiding a career in law, Benjamin became a novelist before entering politics where he was destined to become Prime Minister during the reign of Queen Victoria. Despite this rise to prominence he retained a love of the Chilterns, buying his own Georgian manor in the next valley at Hughenden. This he re-fashioned in the Victorian Gothic tastes of the time and it is now owned by the National Trust. Fortunately no such alterations were made at Bradenham.*

The church, St Botolph, has the typical country parish church amalgam of different periods of architecture, with the early Norman doorway being particularly fine. In addition to commemorating Isaac Disraeli the church also has a chapel named after the Windsors who were earlier occupants of the manor. In 1576 Queen Elizabeth visited the third Lord Windsor there.

Climb the track to the right of Bradenham Manor, which from

Bradenham Manor

the side appears to have more glass than brick in its construction. Follow the track, which divides and then rejoins as it climbs, and go on past a flint cottage to where the the track swings right to Bradenham Hill Farm. Leave it here to continue straight on, to the right of a large holly bush, for a few metres to a Y-junction marked with blue arrows. Fork left, along the route which follows the line of the power cables through the trees, and passing to the right of one small pond continue on to a second. A few metres beyond this is another junction, by a National Trust sign. Turn right here away from the power cables into the trees before swinging left along a wide but indistinct track to the edge of the woods, by the gate to stables. Turn right to a junction of tracks and roads and then go on along the rough road between the houses and the woods until a footpath to the left, signposted "no bicycles", leads between hedges to the main road.

Over the road, cross the stile to the right of Moseley Lodge and go on to a stile in the far right corner of the field. Cross the large field ahead, passing a clump of bushes, to a gap in the hedge to the next field and turn left over the stile and then diagonally to the right across the field to a stile into a wood. A clear path leads through the wood but as it descends and bends to the left look for a smaller path off to the right, opposite a small hollow. This path drops the short distance to a stile at the edge of the wood. Go diagonally to the left, across the field, to reach the road and then right along this to a junction. Turn left, towards Speen, and along the road through the heart of the charming old Upper North Dean, nestling at the junction of a couple of valleys. *It's apt that the influential sculptor Eric Gill and his group dedicated to "Art and the Simple Life" should choose to live and work in an old farmhouse above the village during the 1930s.*

At the top end of the village, take the footpath up the track to the left of the telephone box and village hall. Over the stile by the gate cut left to a second stile into a field and then veer right to another stile by a water trough as the route starts to follow the line of the valley floor. A line of trees leads to the next stile in this delightfully quiet valley, apparently miles from anywhere. Crossing a pair of stiles at the bottom corner of a wood keep to the fence along the right-hand edge of the next field into the right of two possible valleys. After another stile, the valley becomes deeper and more confined as a few of the houses of Speen appear on the skyline to the right. Keep along the bottom, past a stile (across which is a short cut to The Plough, a fine pub once run by the daughter of the Prime Minister Ramsey Macdonald), to turn left through a gate by farm sheds and cross over stiles to the road at Flowers Bottom.

Across the road, climb the stile marked with a white arrow and ascend to a second stile and open fields. Follow the side of the valley climbing up above a few scrubby bushes towards the flint house that can be seen at the top. The view back down the valley whilst climbing is excellent. At the top cross the stile and go left up a concrete path past garages to the junction of roads and turn right. After Flowers Bottom this area goes under the more prosaic name of Turnip End. The road ends shortly at the entrance to two cottages, including Dawn Cottage, just before which there is a footpath over a stile to the left, leading to another stile at the far right corner of the small field. The next field is considerably larger and the path may be indistinct, cross it diagonally to the right aiming just to the right of some large barns on the edge of Lacey Green seen in the distance, to cross a stile in the fence. Then turn left along the edge of the next field and continue straight on over a series of stiles until eventually, past playing fields and school, reaching the road at Lacey Green.

Go to the right along the road and then turn left along Church Lane, passing the church of St John the Evangelist with its large rectangular windows. Follow this road, passing both new and old houses, and past one footpath signposted off to the left to a second by Lane Farm. A few metres down the drive cross the stile by a metal gate into a field often used as a caravan site. Go along the right-hand side of this field to the next stile at the edge of a steep valley, in which Promised Land Farm is hidden from the outside world, and across which is Callows Hill. Drop straight down the valley side to a stile and the farm road running along the valley bottom.

A few metres to the right up the road, turn back left and ascend the track which climbs Callows Hill. At the top a stile gives access to the field ahead with good views across the valley to Lodge Hill backed by Bledlow Ridge as well as the wide sweep of the vale of Aylesbury to the right. Follow the edge of the field round to the left to a stile and a junction of paths. Keep to the fence on the left, to a stile and trees, and take the footpath in the strip of trees and holly running along the top of the hill. Emerging into a field keep to a grassy path, on the right-hand side of a hedge, which follows the bends of the ridge down to meet a small road near the hamlet of Small Dean Farm. *The industrial estate seen in the valley during the descent appears out of place in such a rural setting but is the legacy of the war when the protected valley site was used for an ammunition factory. The Chilterns still have a military significance, indeed this walk encircles the HQ of Strike Command and the Air Force although never within sight of it.*

Go left along the road, briefly, before turning right off it just before a black barn, which also acts as a gate house. Passing between barns follow the grassy track, through an area of newly planted trees, to a large field. Follow the left-hand edge of the field as it curves round beneath woods. At the end turn left and continue to follow the edge of the woods up the valley side and then round to the right to a junction of ways. Keep straight on, past a "National Trust No Riding" sign and, along a grassy track between fields offering some of the best views of Bradenham. The grassy track, after crossing a farm track, leads on to reach Bradenham by the youth hostel opposite the church and green.

WALK 18
West Wycombe - Bradenham
(6km, 3³/₄ miles)

MAPS: O.S. 1:25,000 Pathfinder Sheet 1138
        O.S. 1:50,000 Landranger Sheets 165 and 175
        Chiltern Society Footpath Map No. 7

West Wycombe's history is very much linked to that of one family, the Dashwoods, a family of Dorset yeoman farmers who became silk traders and moved into West Wycombe in 1698. However much of the appearance of the house and locality is due to Sir Francis Dashwood, the Second Lord le Despencer. At the age of 18 Francis was sent, upon his father's death in 1724, on a grand tour of Europe where he acquired a great love of Italian art and architecture. This love came to be reflected in the many architectural projects he undertook around the house, the gardens and the church of West Wycombe. The house and gardens now belong to the National Trust.

Another outcome of Sir Francis's love of Italian art was the founding of the Dilettanti Society, in 1732 or 1733, with others of a similar disposition. This society is still flourishing, which is more than can be said for his most famous, or perhaps, infamous society, The Knights of St Francis of Wycombe commonly known as the "Hell-Fire Club". Started in the 1740s the Hell-Fire Club took up residence in the old Cistercian abbey six miles away at Medmenham on the River Thames. Here the members who included the First Lord of the Admiralty (the Earl of Sandwich), nine MPs, doctors, professors, the son of the Archbishop of Canterbury, and William Hogarth the painter met twice a year for chapter meetings as well as "private devotions". The goings on at the club have become the source of much speculation but probably involved women, drink and irreverence to the Catholic Church rather than Devil worship. Certainly ladies taken there by the brethren were regarded as wives within the walls, and the offspring of such liaisons looked after as the "Sons and Daughters of St Francis". Sir Francis himself had several children by mistresses. The club only became public knowledge as a result of a political argument between John Wilkes, a member and an MP, and the government of Lord Bute which included the Earl of Sandwich and Sir Francis. This lead to Wilkes

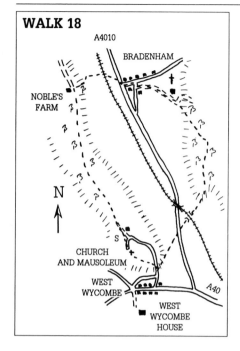

WALK 18

A4010

BRADENHAM

NOBLE'S FARM

N

S

CHURCH AND MAUSOLEUM

WEST WYCOMBE

A40

WEST WYCOMBE HOUSE

imprisonment after insulting King George III, resulting in an outcry at his arrest without trial, as well as the leaking of secrets about Medmenham to undermine the government.

Apart from these activities Sir Francis served in government, as the Post Master-General, and had a philanthropic side to his character. An example of this are the caves at West Wycombe which were basically dug in order to create jobs. Also, improbably considering his founding of the Hell-Fire Club, he was involved in a revision of the Common Book of Prayer. Due to his friendship with Benjamin Franklin this had a greater response in America than England. He died in 1781 leaving no legitimate heir and so was succeeded by his half brother John.

From the top of West Wycombe Hill, with its church and mausoleum set in the remains of an Iron Age fort, this walk follows the crest of the broad wooded ridge beside the Princes Risborough gap. Dropping down to the charming village of Bradenham, with its green and manor house, the walk then returns in the attractive woods on the other side of the valley. The walk is completed either with a tour of West Wycombe village or a more direct climb back up the hill to the start.

START (827,951): The car park at the top of West Wycombe Hill signposted off the A40 at the west end of West Wycombe village. Or start in the village and climb the hill to the church.

PUBLIC TRANSPORT: West Wycombe is on a number of bus routes from High Wycombe and Aylesbury.

ROUTE: Head away from the church, taking the obvious track to the left of Windyhaugh House. Passing through a gate the track leads through an area of selective felling of beech trees, a reminder of Wycombe's foundation upon the furniture industry. A by-product of the felling has been to open up the views from the ridge. Keep to the major track, taking the right fork at a Y-junction, which crosses to the eastern side of the ridge and glimpses of Bradenham. Again follow the main track straight on at a cross-junction.

Unexpectedly the track leads past the front of a flint and brick house, Nobles Farm. Across the track from the buildings a large beech tree has been painted with a number of white arrows. Take the path, off to the right before the tree, which starts descending directly down the slope by a chicken wire fence before bending left by a beech tree painted with an arrow. Cross the stile, to emerge from the woods into an area of pasture and scrub with good views of Bradenham. Bend to the right and drop down to a stile at the bottom. Cross the field beyond to a white painted stile and cross over the railway tracks with care. Go through another small field to a kissing gate and the A4010 road.

Turn right, along the road, to the Red Lion pub and then go to the left up Bradenham Woods Lane. Bradenham is a delightful village, largely consisting of a single row of cottages beside a large green with a church and manor house, which was once the home of Isaac Disraeli, at the top. (For further information about the church and house see Walk 17.)

Leave Bradenham by the gravel road up to the right of the manor. Glimpses over the garden wall suggest the manor house is built more of glass than brick. At the top end of the wall, a few feet before the road divides, a footpath, marked by white arrows, goes off into the trees on the right. Climbing past the edge of a hollow it then bends to the right in the beech woods, running parallel to a field below. Take the left option at a faint Y-fork, indicated by an arrow

Pond in Burnham Beeches (walk 22)
Hedgerley Green (walk 23)

Bluebells near Hellcorner, Ibstone (walk 25)

Woods on Turville Hill (walks 25 & 26)

on a fallen tree across the path. The route is then well marked by white arrows and the number 10, although in crossing a valley a certain amount of initiative is required as whether to go over, under or round the many fallen trees lying across the path.

At the top a T-junction is reached, by a large oak tree and surrounded by numerous arrows on nearby trees. Turn right and follow the path as it traverses above the Wycombe-Bradenham valley through a mixture of beech trees, holly bushes, old clearings with young ash trees, and numerous detours around wind toppled trees. After a while the path passes a group of tall conifers, which are all dead and either gaunt and bare or festooned with ivy. The path then starts to descend gently, through a mixture of conifers and yew trees, until nearing fields on the left it drops more steeply. Eventually running between two wire fences it leads to a gate at the bottom and the railway.

Over the railway the path, usually visible in the crops, veers slightly to the left across the valley bottom to a stile and the A4010 road. Across the road a white arrow indicates a path continuing the same left trend up the field to the top left corner. Looking down to the left "the pedestal", a stone pillar marking the completion of the road to West Wycombe, built in 1752 as a work creation scheme of Sir Francis Dashwood, can be seen. Leaving the field there is the option, either to turn down the road to the village, or to climb the road the short distance to a path on the left leading up the hill towards the mausoleum, the church and the start.

The village displays a rare homogeneity of largely un-spoilt sixteenth-to eighteenth-century buildings, with examples of old coaching houses, furniture factories, as well as different housing. Bought by the Royal Society of Arts the village is now in the ownership of the National Trust. From the village there are a number of obvious routes up the hill to the caves, mausoleum and church.

Completed in 1765 the vast open-air flint mausoleum repeats, but on a much grander scale, the design used for the archway of the Temple of Apollo, in the grounds of the house. It was built using a £500 legacy left by George Dudington, a member of the club, whose name is included with Dashwood's in a frieze. The heart of another Hell Fire Club member, Paul Whitehead a poet, was set into the walls. The choice of site for a monument to vanity could not have been better, dominating as it does the valley from

Dashwood Mausoleum, West Wycombe

High Wycombe. Footpaths either side of the mausoleum lead to the church set in the earthworks of an Iron Age fort called Haveringdon, or "the hill of Heafer's people". The start is the other side of the church

The Church of St Lawrence, despite being medieval, now appears overwhelmingly Georgian after alterations by Sir Francis Dashwood. What was once a Norman tower is now crowned by a gilded ball 8ft in diameter. Erected in 1751 it is similar to the Ball of Fortune, on a tower by the Grand Canal in Venice, which Sir Francis must have visited on his travels. The interior of the ball (a small admission charge) was described by Wilkes as "the best globe tavern I was ever in". Sir Francis also used the porthole in the ball to signal, by heliograph, to his friend John Norris, who had erected an identical ball in Camberley, 34 miles away.

His love of continental architecture also led Sir Francis Dashwood to have the interior of the main body of the church redecorated in the style of the Temple of Bel at Palmyra. The columns, stucco, decorated ceiling, and marble floors combine in a richness unique among the charmingly simple churches of the Chilterns.

WALK 19
Wheeler End - Towerage
(6.5km, 4 miles)

MAPS: O.S. 1:25,000 Pathfinder Sheet 1138
       O.S. 1:50,000 Landranger Sheet 175
       Chiltern Society Footpath Map No. 7 (and 11 for few
       metres only)

Situated on the edge of High Wycombe between the A40 and M40 this is a surprisingly quiet walk. From Wheeler End the route follows along the top of the valley, with good views of West Wycombe Hill, to Towerage above West Wycombe House. The return to Wheeler End is by a secluded wooded valley.

START (803,931): Wheeler End Common by the Brickmaker's Arms. This is reached either from the A40, turning off by the Dashwood Arms on the edge of Piddington, or from the B482 Marlow to Stokenchurch road turning off by The Peacock in Bolter End.

PUBLIC TRANSPORT: Infrequent buses to Wheeler End from High Wycombe.

ROUTE: From the Brickmaker's Arms go obliquely to the left, across the corner of the common, to the gravel road and up Piddington Lane which leads off this part way along the side of the common. Opposite the gate to Woodman's Nap cross the stile on the right and follow the hedge parallel to the road. At an opening in the fence cross the road and stile opposite before continuing parallel to the road again. It would be easier just to follow the road but this route is safer than walking along the narrow road confined between banks and also the higher elevation of the fields gives better viewpoints of the surrounding country including the early eighteenth-century Chipp's Manor away to the left and West Wycombe Church straight ahead. A stile by Warwick Lodge brings a final return to the road.

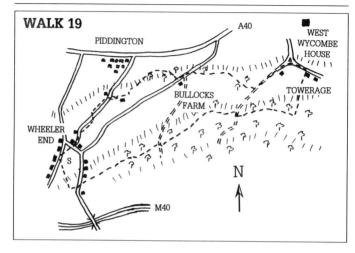

Cross the road and go up the grassy lane opposite to a stile into a field by a farm with a number of barn conversions. Keep straight on through the field along the top edge with views down to Piddington below. Cross the stile at the end of the field and turn left down the edge of the next field to a gate into the woods. A path descends through the beech woods tending to the right. Keep following the same trend through a recently felled area (hopefully replanted by now) to a stile at the bottom.

Do not cross this stile but start to climb diagonally back up again, to a stile and a plantation of young trees and conifers. Go straight through these to another stile and track. A few metres to the left along this a road is reached by Bullocks Farm, which possesses a splendid flint barn.

Start down the road to the left, with views of West Wycombe church picturesquely framed by trees, but take care not to miss the path up the bank and through the woods on the right. Cross the stile and turn left along the edge of the field. Pass through a gap to a lower field and follow the hedge on the right along its top edge to a stile into woods. A path leads slightly to the right at first through the woods to a field which is then crossed to a white stile opposite. The field occupies the crest of a ridge, with Bullocks Farm to the right and Towerage to the left. Go through the bushes to a pair of farm tracks and, crossing the first, turn left along the second and then along by the hedge. This track runs along the top of the ridge past a pylon with views of the seemingly distant houses of High Wycombe and the deep wooded valley down to the right which is the return route to Wheeler End. Follow the now gravel road past Towerage Cottage and keep to the right at the junction where the road to West Wycombe drops off to the left.

Shortly past the junction is a gap in the trees on the left with the somewhat unexpected appearance of an equestrian statue. *The statue is at the head of a recently remade ride, originally dating from the 1750s, leading to the south front of West Wycombe House which owes a lot of its design to Sir Francis Dashwood's love of Italian architecture (see Walk 18 for a history of the Dashwoods). The statue, however, is modern fibreglass bought from Pinewood Studios but nevertheless very effective.*

A few metres along the road, after the statue, cross a stile to the right of the thatched cottage, and go along the left hand side of a field. The path starts to drop through an area of brambles and bushes to a cross-junction, turn right here and cross the stile. Descend through small trees to a stile over a wire fence. The path then traverses along secluded in an area dense with young trees including a lot of ash trees. Keep to the main path, for quite a distance, until meeting a forest track and turn right uphill on this for a few metres to where it bends right. Turn off this to the left on a faint path, which is confirmed as the correct way by a white arrow painted on a beech tree a few metres in. It soon becomes a better established path in older woods containing a high proportion of distinguished yew trees. In an area of thinner trees keep straight on crossing a path connecting a forest track, running along the valley bottom to the left, and a field to the right. Keep following the white arrows bisecting the trees between the track and the field.

The path comes to an end at a track near the edge of the wood, turn right along this for a couple of metres to a T-junction and then turn left keeping straight on along the path in a strip of trees between fields. Fork right beneath a large oak tree to follow the path leading along a shallow valley with the old beech trees of Denham Wood. Cross the stile at the end of the woods into an open field with the houses of Wheeler End on the skyline and continue along the valley to a stile near two tall conifer trees. Pass between the garden fences to reach the road. Turn left down the road to the valley bottom again and then turn right onto the common along a path beside the bye-law notices. Turn right into the obvious gap in the bushes and hawthorn trees and climb up to the open grass and on to the start.

WALK 20
Penn - Forty Green
(6.4km, 4 miles)

MAPS: O.S. 1:25,000 Pathfinder Sheet 1138
           O.S. 1:50,000 Landranger Sheet 175
           Chiltern Society Footpath Map Nos. 6 and 13

Located in the open land between High Wycombe and Beaconsfield the walk is centred around the long straggling village of Penn. Passing through Forty Green, which has connections with Charles II, the walk is particularly attractive in early summer when the orchards there are in bloom.

Penn is one of the Chiltern names to have created a niche in history through the family of that name. Sybil Penn was the governess to Queen Elizabeth I and was given Penn House and the right in perpetuity to appoint the vicar of Holy Trinity Church, Penn, as a wedding present by King Henry VIII. It was William Penn (1644-1718), though, who became the most famous member of the family. Adopting Quakerism and persecuted for preaching about it he sought escape by securing from Charles II the grant and charter of Pennsylvania, named by the king in honour of William's father who had been a loyal admiral and even lent the king £16000. It was intended that Pennsylvania and Philadelphia, 'the city of brotherly love', which Penn founded, should be a holy experiment based upon Quaker principles. Not all went to plan, however, and he was forced to spend time in an English debtor's jail and was on the point of surrendering Pennsylvania to the crown when apoplexy struck in 1712. William Penn is buried, along with other Quaker luminaries at nearby Jordan's Quaker

Church which also claims to have a barn constructed with timber from the
pilgrim ship the Mayflower.

START (907,937): The Red Lion, Penn, on the B474 Beaconsfield to
Tyler Green road opposite the Kingswood road junction and village
green. Parking in the vicinity is a little limited.

An alternative parking spot is near Penn Church further along
the B474 towards Beaconsfield, starting the walk there.

PUBLIC TRANSPORT: Bus service to start of walk in Penn from
High Wycombe (not Sundays).

ROUTE: Take the track to the left of the Red Lion pub, through open
farmland, to Puttenham Place Farm, a large solitary brick house
with stone mushrooms in the garden. *These staddles, as they are
properly known, now decorate many a Chiltern garden but were originally
used as stilts upon which
granaries were built, the
mushroom shape being
designed to keep mice out.*
In order to pass the
house turn left and
follow the edge of
fields round to the back
of the farm, turning
right then left to
continue more or less

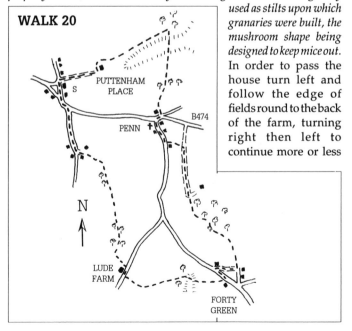

in the original direction along the left-hand side of a field which dips away to form a valley. The silhouette of Penn Church stands prominently on the ridge across the valley. Continue on to a T-junction by a wood and turn away from the wood crossing the valley and the track at its bottom and up the other side to a stile leading into woods. Veering slightly left, a distinct path leads up through the wood, exiting at the top to run along by the fence of a pub garden and across stiles to the B474 Beaconsfield to Tyler Green road, by The Crown, an old ivy clad building part of which was once a coffin-maker's shop.

Almost opposite The Crown is Holy Trinity Church, Penn, a largely flint church that has been maintained by the Penn and Curzon families since it was given as a gift to Sybil Penn by Henry VIII. Much of it is older than that, dating back to the eleventh century with a fifteenth-century tower. Locals have claimed twelve different counties can be seen from the tower, a claim owing much to the church's location on a ridge of the Chilterns as well as good eyesight and perhaps a little imagination. Inside the church there are many interesting artifacts including a Norman lead font and old brasses commemorating the Penn family. The most unusual relic, though, which was only re-discovered during work on the roof in 1938, is the Penn Doom. One of only five examples in the country the doom is a fifteenth-century painting on oak boards depicting the last judgement and is now to be seen above the chancel arch.

One offspring of a respectable Penn family not honoured in the church, although his father was a churchwarden, is Jack Shrimpton (1672-1713). After time spent as an apprentice soap boiler and then in the army Jack Shrimpton took to crime, becoming a notorious highwayman working the London to Oxford road near Gerrards Cross. Leading a double life he dined with respectable people one day only to rob them the next taking as much as £150 in a day. There was, however, nothing glamorous about his death being hung for shooting a watchman whilst drunk.

From the church follow the minor road, Paul's Hill, which, passing a few cottages starts to descend rapidly. Just before the gates to the vicarage leave the road on the left, by the footpath signpost, and climb the bank and broken stile. Follow the edge of the field next to the vicarage hedge and then go straight on between two open fields to a metalled farm road. Turn right along the road, but where it turns off to Underwood, continue along in the same direction on a footpath between beech woods and a hedge. Entering a strand of conifers the path veers to the right and then shortly to the left. Keep to the main path, passing a path off to the right, through the woods which develop into a mature beech wood until, just after another path joins from the left, a stile gives access to a small field on the right. A series of stiles leads downhill to a drive by houses. Turn immediately right onto a path between hawthorns which leads past garages and houses to The Royal Standard of England.

This inn is built in a marvellous jumble of bricks, timbers and low tiled roofs. It is in these roofs that the story has it Charles II hid during his escape to France after the Battle of Worcester in 1651. After the restoration of the monarchy the unique name of The Royal Standard of England was bestowed upon the inn by Charles II in gratitude. Nowadays the inn is also renowned for its selection of cheese and pies and hence can be busy at peak periods.

At the road junction by the inn turn left down the hill to a signposted footpath and a stile, just before a group of houses on the right. Entering an orchard there is no worn path to follow but keeping parallel to the left-hand fence a granary barn, converted into a summer house with windows but still on its staddles, can be seen in the field to the left. (Restored examples of granary barns can be seen at the Chiltern Open Air Museum, see Appendix B.) Descend diagonally to the right down the slope to a stile near power cable posts. Over the stile keep to the right-hand edge of the field, which forms the bottom of a valley, and up to the corner to meet another footpath. Turn left here and follow the path through the mixed scrub and trees, passing a path off to the right, to the edge of the trees above another valley which has good views towards Beaconsfield Church spire. Go straight across the field and valley to the other side, turning right at the top to follow a hedge until crossing a stile to the left a small field leads to the road at Lude Farm. Once again Penn Church is to be seen on the skyline.

A few metres to the right along the road there is a stile into the field beyond the farm buildings. In the field aim for the stile at the end of the woods across the field and then turning right cross a second stile into the woods and fork left immediately at a Y-junction marked with arrows. Through the dark conifers a wider path joins from the right and the woods become no more than a narrow strip.

Penn green and pond

At the end of the trees keep straight on by the edge of a field and over a stile follow the path through an area of trees and hawthorn bushes. Go along the left-hand edge of the next field to a stile often guarded by a muddy pool and then by a wire fence towards a bungalow. Crossing a final stile a drive leads shortly to a road servicing the houses of this section of Penn village. Go right along the road to meet the busier B474 and turning left along this a short road through a cluster of antique shops cuts the corner back to the start.

WALK 21
Coleshill - Winchmore Hill
(8.9km, 5¹/₂ miles)

MAPS: O.S. 1:25,000 Pathfinder Sheet 1138
          O.S. 1:50,000 Landranger Sheets 165 and 175
          Chiltern Society Footpath Map No. 6

Between Amersham and Beaconsfield lies a ridge upon which the villages of Coleshill and Winchmore Hill are situated. Compared to the valleys either side these have remained relatively undeveloped. This walk links the two as well as the attractive countryside around them.

START (959,942): The Forestry Commission picnic area Hodgemoor Woods which is off to the left from the Chalfont St Giles road off the A355 Amersham to Beaconsfield road.

PUBLIC TRANSPORT: Limited bus service to Coleshill from Amersham and Uxbridge (not Sundays). Join walk at the Red Lion pub in Coleshill.

ROUTE: Follow the unmade road through the picnic area until at the edge of the woods where it bends right back towards the Chalfont St Giles road. Turn left here to follow a footpath along the right-hand side of a field, from where Coleshill Windmill, a tower-mill built in 1856 and visible from various points on the walk, can be seen on the skyline to the left. Follow the edge of the field round to the left to a stile hidden in the hedge and then, keeping to the edge of the next field, go round a clump of trees to the start of a series of stiles. These lead to a footpath beside a row of stately oak trees along the left-hand edge of a field and down to the A355 road.

    Across the road, a path drops down the steep bank to a large oak tree and then goes straight on by the hedge of the right-hand field. Gently climb to the trees ahead and then turn right to follow the edge bending round to the left to a corner of the field. The path

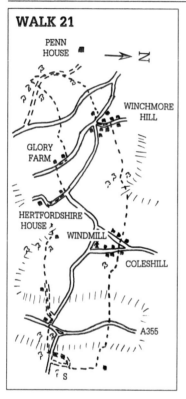

WALK 21

PENN HOUSE

N

WINCHMORE HILL

GLORY FARM

HERTFORDSHIRE HOUSE

WINDMILL

COLESHILL

A355

S

continues straight on climbing between two old hedges to reach the village of Coleshill by the Red Lion pub.

Coleshill is still very much as a village should be with its church, pond and village store all in close proximity. The village is also noted as the home of Edmund Waller, a famous orator and poet at the time of the Civil War. His loyalties, though, tended to fluctuate and when sent by Parliament to Oxford in 1643 as one of the commissionaires to negotiate with Charles I he returned and tried to seize London for the king. He was only saved from the gallows by incriminating his associates. Later his poems praising Cromwell led to a reconcilement with Parliament, but this did not stop him from being equally full of praise for Charles II upon the restoration.

From the Red Lion take the footpath opposite, between Stoney Path Cottage and the church, to another road and across this along the drive towards Lands Farm. Where the drive divides go through the right-hand gate and along by the brick wall to a stile and then a short section of concrete road to another stile. Follow the left-hand edge of the field to a stile into the next field and turn left here for a few metres before veering right and descending past a small group of trees to the recessed corner of a mature beechwood. A clear path cuts through this narrow wood bending right then left at the far side to follow the hedge along the left-hand side of a field and beneath power cables. In the distance the spire of Penn Street Church can be seen, unusual in that few churches in the Chilterns have spires. Follow the edge of the next field to the corner where a footpath leads on between hedges, to the left of a small factory, to the road at Winchmore Hill opposite the Methodist Chapel.

Turn left along the road to the Plough Inn, at the road junction. Then cross the green, between the High Wycombe and Penn roads, aiming to the right of the majority of the houses, to find a stile tucked away in the hedge. Cross straight over the field to a small road and, over this and the stile, keep left at a junction. Passing a sign warning "loose dogs are at risk" follow the footpath in a strip of beech trees and rhododendrons. Reaching a metalled drive turn left along it to where it bends to the left and a signposted footpath leads off to the right. To keep to the rights of way follow this to a vermin control sign and turn back left on a smaller path marked with white arrows to return to the drive only a few metres from where it was left. Across the drive a footpath is marked by white arrows along near the left-hand edge off the trees to a stile and coniferous trees. Continue until exiting from woods pass to the left of a hollow and then cross the field towards an area of short trees to the left of a large solitary oak tree.

Cross the minor road and the stile opposite to a footpath between a hedge and the area of short trees, which is an overgrown orchard. Follow the right-hand edge of the field beyond to a stile on the right, before a group of trees, and along the edge of the adjacent field past the trees. Then turn left, through a gap, and go along by the hedge ahead passing below power cables. Reaching a farm track cross the stile by a tree ahead and then a second towards the farm, Glory Farm. Immediately turn left along by the fence down and right to a stile, noting the granary barn of the farm. Cross the small field past the water trough and turn right down the road. Follow the road down to Lowlands, a brick and timber house, where at the end of a grassy ramp to the left of the road is a stile and footpath. Climb alongside the hedge on the right to the crest of the ridge, in sight of the windmill again, and a road.

Turn right, along the road to a junction, and then right again down a minor road. Before the road bends right by a large house turn left on a footpath through a gate and stile. *The house is called Hertfordshire House which may seem a little odd being so far inside the boundaries of Buckinghamshire but is explained by the fact that Coleshill was once a detached island of Hertfordshire within Bucks. This was utilised by Thomas Ellwood, who held illegal Quaker meetings at his home in the area, being outside the jurisdiction of Buckinghamshire but too remote for the Hertfordshire magistrates to bother about.* Drop down to the stile, at the bottom left corner of the field, and up the green track beyond to a kissing gate and a good view back to Hertfordshire House. Cross the field diagonally to the right, past a house, to an old metal gate and then down by the hedge to the left. Go straight on along the footpath marked with white arrows through the trees. Turn left and climb up by the edge of the field beyond passing below power cables to a stile over the fence to the left of a white farmhouse. Take the farm road ahead and to the left of the farmhouse. This drops down to a road and turn right down this to the A355 by The Magpies pub.

Cross the road and a few metres to the left a footpath is signposted across a stile into the beechwoods. The path climbs past pits to a junction; veer left here and descend to an area for car parking. To the left across the road is the picnic area.

WALK 22
Burnham Beeches - Littleworth Common
(7km, 4¹/₂ miles)

MAPS: O.S. 1:25,000 Pathfinder Sheet 1157
O.S. 1:50,000 Landranger Sheet 175
Not covered by Chiltern Society Footpath Map

Burnham Beeches is much more complicated than the monoculture its name would suggest. Areas of heathland, bog, pine and birch are to be found in addition to the beech trees. However the older beech trees, some 350 years old, represent one of the oldest surviving managed woodlands in the country. Cut regularly at about eight feet the pollarded trees provided a source of fuel wood. The reason for pollards as opposed to coppicing (cutting at ground level) was to keep the new shoots out of reach of livestock. With coal becoming more readily available the practice of lopping the trees stopped about 1820, allowing them to grow to their current grotesque forms. In 1880 Burnham Beeches was bought by the Corporation of London, as an open space for public recreation. This was not exactly to the liking of the locals who regarded Burnham Beeches as their own and threw the first head keeper into a pond. Burnham Beeches has had many devotees including Jenny Lind, Felix Mendelssohn and Thomas Gray who described the venerable beeches as "dreaming out their old stories to the winds". Today there is much conservation work going on to maintain and rejuvenate the beeches.

Using the network of numerous paths and drives within Burnham Beeches this walk starts and finishes there but also crosses the open country to the village of Littleworth Common, passing Dorneywood House en route.

START (955,851): Lord Mayors Drive, East Burnham Common. This is reached from the A355 Beaconsfield to Slough road turning off on to Beeches Road in Farnham Common Village (signposted to Burnham Beeches). This meets the edge of East Burnham Common almost at the start of Lord Mayors Drive. There are plenty of parking spaces beside the drive before reaching Victory Cross.

PUBLIC TRANSPORT: Buses from Slough to Farnham Common and follow Beeches Road.

ROUTE: Wander along the common, beside the road and past the refreshments kiosk, to the cross-roads at Victory Cross. Leaving the roads here take the trodden path, behind the wooden shelter on the left, to continue parallel to the drive. Passing to the left of a rhododendron bush keep straight on for a few metres to find a path at right angles to the left which drops straight down the slope before bending to the right at the bottom beside the Upper Pond. Follow the path along the edge of the pond to the junction at the dam, and go straight on along a smaller path keeping to the right of the small stream which flows into a marshy area and then another pond, the Lower Pond. *The stream was first dammed about 1800 to create the ponds which were used for washing sheep until 1883.* By the dam there is another junction; turn right here to climb the main path keeping

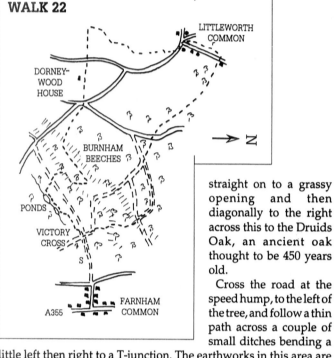

WALK 22

LITTLEWORTH COMMON

DORNEY-WOOD HOUSE

BURNHAM BEECHES

PONDS

VICTORY CROSS

FARNHAM COMMON

A355

→ N

straight on to a grassy opening and then diagonally to the right across this to the Druids Oak, an ancient oak thought to be 450 years old.

Cross the road at the speed hump, to the left of the tree, and follow a thin path across a couple of small ditches bending a little left then right to a T-junction. The earthworks in this area are thought to be part of an Iron Age enclosure. Turn right along the path, which is shortly joined by another from the left, and passing some holly bushes drops down a slight hollow to a junction of paths. Turn left, downhill past the pollarded beech, and keep straight on down past a turning off to the left after a few metres. Bits of an old wire fence run beside the path which bends to the right keeping close to holly bushes and then down to the valley floor.

Turn left along the track, Victoria Drive, among large beeches and following the valley floor. After a while a small earth ridge boundary can be seen on the right and at a cross-junction of paths turn right to follow this earth ridge which also bends here. The path climbs, keeping to the left of the ridge, and passing a holly bush go straight on at a junction through some birch trees before more oak and beech trees. Crossing a small channel the trees thin out and take one of the several paths to reach the road on the left.

Turn right to the road junction of Green Lane and Curriers Lane and turn left on a footpath signposted across a stile into a field, just past the driveway to Juniper Hill. Follow the left-hand edge of the field across a gentle valley. On the climb up Dorneywood House can be seen to the left. *This was built early this century on the site of an old farmhouse and left to the nation by Lord Courtauld Thompson for use by government ministers, often the Chancellor of the Exchequer.*

At the end of the field cross the stiles to the road and into the field beyond heading towards the left-hand end of a group of trees. By the trees the path meets a bridleway but turn right and cross the stile to leave it immediately again. Through the bushes into the field follow the right-hand edge, by a row of oak trees, and pass between holly trees into the next field. Bending right then left follow the edge of the field with views up to a large brick house in Littleworth Corner. Ignore the stile to the right and go on to reach the end of the next field and then up between trees to another field. Again turn right to follow the edge of the field round almost three sides to a gap in the bushes and a stile to the road. Turn left along the road to the junction in front of The Beech Tree pub.

A few metres beyond Common Lane, turn right along a footpath that follows the line of cables through the birch covered common. At the junction of wires the path turns left then right to a car park in front of the Blackwood Arms. A footpath is signposted as the Beeches Way to the right of Woodside and across stiles to follow the right-hand side of a field by trees. At the stile at the end veer right across the next field to enter trees via a gate. Keep straight on, as another path joins from the right, and follow the occasionally waymarked main path through the trees.

Cross the stile to the road and go along the track opposite through rhododendrons to the road, Morton Drive, and turn left at the road junction onto McAuliffe Drive. *Very shortly on the left are the remains of Hartley Court Moat, a medieval moated farm homestead. The inner enclosure and moat seen here protected the houses from the livestock whilst the outer defensive bank is crossed a little further on at a speed hump.* Keep on the quiet road, through oaks and golden azaleas, until it reaches a T-junction. Leave the roads here to go straight on down the slope on what becomes a clear track, Burnham Walk. The track crosses a small stream, which disappears into a sink on the left, and then goes on to a junction. Make a right-angled turn to the left onto a path leading down to cross another stream before climbing up through the trees, heading a little to the right, to find a track crossing the slope. Turn right along this, continuing on as another joins, to pass through some rhododendrons to reach a road. Turn left along the road for the short distance back to Victory Cross.

WALK 23
Fulmer - Hedgerley
(9km, 5¹/₂ miles)

MAPS: O.S. 1:25,000 Pathfinder Sheet 1157
O.S. 1:50,000 Landranger Sheet 175
Not covered.by Chiltern Society Footpath Map

This route connects the picturesque villages of Fulmer and Hedgerley who deservedly seem to alternately win the title of the best kept village in Buckinghamshire. Although part of the walk is within sight of the M40, the motorway never becomes so obtrusive as to ruin the scenery. On the return leg the route crosses Stoke Common, an unusual place which in bad weather is more reminiscent of Culloden Moor in Scotland than the Chilterns.

START (999,857): By Fulmer Church. The village of Fulmer is reached by minor roads from Gerrards Cross, Stoke Poges or Slough. Parking in the village is easiest along Hay Lane which is opposite the church and Black Horse pub.

PUBLIC TRANSPORT: A limited bus service runs to Fulmer from Slough (not on Sundays).

ROUTE: *Although enlarged and altered in the late nineteenth century the*

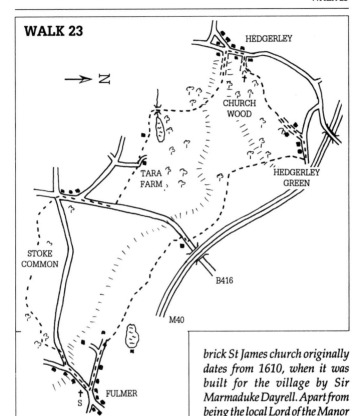

WALK 23

→ N

HEDGERLEY

CHURCH WOOD

TARA FARM

HEDGERLEY GREEN

STOKE COMMON

B416

M40

FULMER

brick St James church originally dates from 1610, when it was built for the village by Sir Marmaduke Dayrell. Apart from being the local Lord of the Manor this benefactor served in the influential position of paymaster for the first two Stuart kings. Sir Marmaduke and his first wife, Dame Anne, are commemorated inside the church by a monument of their effigies lying above the praying figures of their children. This and a wooden Jacobean font are the main features of interest in the church.

From the church go down Hay Lane opposite, passing the fork off left which goes up to Fulmer Hall, the large white building very noticeable from the M40. At the entrance to Fulmer Chase Farm cross the stile, at the right-hand end of the wooden fence, and follow the path along by old metal railings. *To the right is Low Farm, once the site of the village church, and to its side the recently cleared mere, from which Fulmer got its original name Fugelmere, or bird-haunted mere. With time the mere, which had been turned into watercress beds, had silted up to become little more than a marshy area, but now it is once again the haunt of Canada geese and other birds.*

Across a stile go to the end of the field and a junction of paths. Turn right, to the stile, and follow the path, along between hedges, to another stile by the remains of an old kissing gate. Keep straight on, following a track past old gravel workings and under the power cables, to a signposted footpath which runs along beside a row of large pine trees. This leads to the B416 road by Fulmer Valley Farm.

Turn right, towards the underpass under the M40 motorway, but before reaching it turn left along Mount Hill Lane. Over a stile go to the end of the track and cross a stile on the left. Follow the hedge of the field as it runs diagonally to the left away from the motorway. At the corner of the field a junction of paths is marked by white arrows. Cross the stile by a gate and then immediately over another stile, on the right, to climb uphill between a wire fence and a hedge of trees. A distinct path leads through the woods at the top and then on between hedges to a quiet road. Turn left, along the road, to the hamlet of Hedgerley Green which is little more than a handful of houses beside a green and scattered ponds.

By the main pond turn left, onto the bridleway which follows a track along the green. Where the track swings left, to Sherley Close, keep straight on between two rows of trees. The bridleway skirts a wood and, passing a path off to the right, starts to descend towards Hedgerley. Join the drive to St Marys church, a flint church containing some interesting murals but which is usually locked, and descend to the road in the village. *The village was once in the domain of Bulstrode Park, where Judge Jeffries built a house in 1686.*

Turn left, away from The White Horse pub, and go past the Old School Cottage which is decorated with the plaintive inscription "feed my lambs". Between the small village pond and a large Georgian brick house take the track leading off to the left past the tradesman's entrance. *The house, Hedgerley Court Farm, was once used by the "C of E Society for waifs and strays" for training boys in agriculture.* The track ends at a stile, next to a gate, into a delightful meadow set

One of the ponds at Hedgerley Green

in a low wide valley. To the left is Church Wood, an R.S.P.B. reserve for woodland birds. Cross the field, diagonally to the right, to a stile near the opposite corner and ascend through the mixed woods on a distinct path. Over the stile near the top go to the edge of the wood and then straight on along a footpath between a hedge and wire fence. At the end of the fence cross the footbridge over a small stream, feeding a lake in the trees on the left. Cross the stile into the field and turning left cross another stile very shortly. Ahead is Hedgerley Park Farm and, aiming for the left-hand end of these buildings, cross the field. To the left of a railway sleeper and girder construction a stile and path leads behind the buildings to another stile, at the far end beneath a tall conifer tree, and more fields. Past the power cable post, cross the stile and go across the next field to a stile in the hedge and a road leading from Tara Farm, an over beautified house.

At the corner of the road by Tara Stud a footpath leads on

through the bushes to the right of the gate to Tara Stud. Continue along the left-hand hedge of the field beyond to the B416 road. Turn right along the pavement on the other side of the road and past the Fox and Pheasant pub to the junction of the Stoke Poges and Fulmer roads.

This is at the corner of Stoke Common, 200 acres of which were vested in trustees in 1810 to provide fuel for the poor inhabitants, with the lord of the manor forgoing his right to dig brick earth there. It is now a highly complex mosaic of vegetation and ecosystems with areas of woodland, gorse, heather, and young trees, which is often if not always wet whatever the weather. Navigation across the common is never simple, particularly as footpaths seem to appear or disappear quite frequently. For an adventure discover your own selection of paths (and get lost) to return to the Fulmer road at the far end. Or for only marginally less....

Look for a footpath ahead, from the corner of the B416 and Stoke Common Road, through bushes and between log fences designed to keep horses out and marked accordingly. The path bends left, through birch trees, before crossing a ditch and eventually reaching more open ground. Keep to the main path to the next anti-horse barrier, and then bend left, past two isolated pine trees, and go straight past a crossed-out horseshoe sign to the right-hand end of a thinned group of pine trees. Turn left in front of these to reach a gravelled track and turn right along this to a cross-junction of large gravelled bridleways. From the junction looking along the one to the left a house can be seen at its end, take the next one clockwise. A footpath runs a little to its left but soon becomes waterlogged.

Going along by an area of trees continue straight on, at a junction where another gravelled track joins from the left, and on to a Y-junction. Take the right fork, which is as yet not gravelled, to a cross-junction of similar sized paths. Turn left and go through the trees to the road. Turn right along the road to a junction and then left down to Fulmer Church.

WALK 24
Watlington Hill
(5.6km, 3½ miles)

MAPS: O.S. 1:25,000 Pathfinder Sheet 1137
O.S. 1:50,000 Landranger Sheet 175
Chiltern Society Footpath Map No. 9

This short walk connects the viewpoints of Watlington Hill and Watlington Park, on the edge of the Chiltern scarp, via a section of the ancient Icknield Way which runs along the bottom of the scarp.

START (710,936): National Trust car park at the top of Watlington Hill off the Watlington to Christmas Common road.

PUBLIC TRANSPORT: Buses to Watlington and then walk towards Christmas Common to meet the Ridgeway path at the base of the hill.

ROUTE: From the car park follow the dark green arrows first along a grassy strip and then along the footpath by the side of the road towards Watlington. The path bends away from the road, through a kissing gate, to a grassy swathe which leads through bushes and gorse. Climb gently to reach the crest of the ridge, which forms Watlington Hill, near its end. The views from the hill are amongst the best from the Chiltern scarp. Nestling below is the town of Watlington, with the Oxfordshire plains beyond, whilst the eroded scarp continues with Pyrton Hill and Shirburn Hill to the north-east, and down past Swyncombe Downs towards the Thames and Didcot power station to the south-west.

Descend the spur a little to the right towards the town. The descent steepens as it passes the White Mark of Watlington, an obelisk shape cut into the chalk. *Unlike many of the chalk marks whose mystic origins are lost in the history of time this mark is a relatively recent creation. In 1764 Edward Horne, who felt that the church should have a spire, had this proxy spire cut into the chalk on the hill beyond to "fit" onto the church from the viewpoint of his window.*

At the bottom of the mark take the right-hand path at a junction and, passing between hawthorn bushes, cross a stile and follow the path down to the road. Before reaching the houses marking the outskirts of the town turn left along a gravel road signposted to Landscape Caravan Club and less obviously as the Ridgeway footpath. After a short distance take the right hand option at a fork junction and follow the now unmade track. Secluded between the hedgerows and meandering a little as it follows the bottom of the scarp it's hard to think of this quiet track as one of the main trading routes of England, but as one part of the Icknield Way it once was just that. Towards the end of this track Watlington Park, a fine Georgian red-brick house occupying a prominent position on the scarp, can be glimpsed through gaps in the hedgerow to the left.

At the junction with a road turn left, following the road round the bend to the left where a gravel road leads off to the left. Keep to the gravel track, labelled W6, past the junction with the path W7 at a brick pillar surmounted by a stone ball. Continue past the brick house and, keeping to the right at a fork of tracks, follow the track, with fine views of Watlington Hill to the left, until it makes a right-angled turn to the left. Leave the track here to continue straight on along W8, a smaller track, leading through a band of trees to a field. Climb directly up the field towards a gap in the trees on the crest of the scarp.

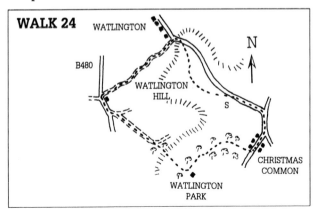

WALK 24 WATLINGTON

B480

WATLINGTON HILL

S

N

CHRISTMAS COMMON

WATLINGTON PARK

Looking down the White Mark of Watlington Hill

At the top of the slope go through the gate into the right-hand group of trees and, almost immediately, turn left to cross the avenue leading from Watlington Park cut into the trees. *Unfortunately only the top floor of the Georgian brick house can be seen. It was built for John Tilson in 1755, on the site of an earlier 1675 house. The earlier house was a second home of the Stonors of Stonor Park who, faced with financial difficulties due to religious persecution, had to sell it. (See Walk 27 for a history of the Stonors.)* Across the avenue follow the clearly marked footpath through the beech woods.

Bending right the footpath exits Lower Dean's Wood and becomes grassier as it passes through an area of mixed trees and shrubs leading to a tarmac driveway. Turn left along the drive to the road near the charming End Lodge and turn left again here, towards the village of Christmas Common. *The name Christmas Common was reputedly bestowed upon the village after a truce was arranged here between the Royalists and the Roundheads for the Christmas of 1643 during the Civil War.* Continuing past the Fox and Hounds pub turn

121

left at the road junction and shortly left again, following the signposts towards Watlington, to return to the car park.

WALK 25
Ibstone - Turville
(11.8km, 7¹/₄ miles)

MAPS: O.S. 1:25,000 Pathfinder Sheet 1137
        O.S. 1:50,000 Landranger Sheet 175
        Chiltern Society Footpath Map Nos. 9 and 11

The large raised common of Ibstone lies on the crest of a ridge running down towards Turville. Rather than following the ridge this walk descends a quiet and secluded adjacent valley before crossing the ridge by Turville Windmill to the picturesque village of Turville. The return is made via the heights of Turville Grange, the isolated small church of Ibstone and the sinister sounding Hell Corner.

START (752,937): The common at Ibstone. This is quickly reached from the Stokenchurch junction on the M40. There is parking opposite The Fox pub and along the edge of the common.

PUBLIC TRANSPORT: Occasional buses to Ibstone from High Wycombe (not Sundays).

ROUTE: Opposite the cricket pitch on the common a track, by the sign "Grimaldes", leads between houses and then along the right-hand side of a field with distant views of Stokenchurch. When the track turns off to a farm on the right keep straight on, along the edge of the field, to the corner and a Y-junction. Turn right (S40) and drop steeply through the bushes and trees in a slight valley. Emerging eventually at the corner of fields keep straight on, by the hedgerow, and then beneath power cables along the footpath through the edge of a conifer wood. Keeping right at a Y-junction the valley bottom is reached at an opening with a grassy track running left to right.

WALK 25

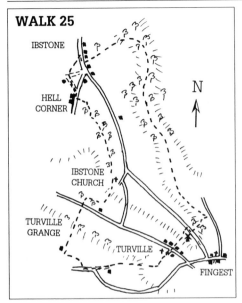

IBSTONE

HELL
CORNER

IBSTONE
CHURCH

TURVILLE
GRANGE

TURVILLE

FINGEST

N

Turn right along this track to follow the valley for some distance. The flora of this section of the valley is one of the most varied in the Chilterns, with many different trees and flowers, and consequently supports a rich fauna, from butterflies to deer.

Keep to the valley base across a marked cross-junction and on in younger trees and later across a track leading to a field on the left from the Harecramp Estate conservation area. Further on the path swings right by a fence to cross a wide gravel track which leads to farm sheds and fields on the left. Cross the track 10 metres to the right of the gate and immediately keep left at a Y-fork, entering a conifer wood after a short distance. Cross the large stile, at the barrier by a gate, into a strip of woodland between fields. Continue straight on the path, marked I14, at a junction and again a few metres later where the main track swings to the right. The next section, in a strip of beech trees, is prone to be muddy but is easily avoided to the sides. At a gate the trees cease but continue down the valley through more gates until a track is reached. Turn sharp right here and cross the stile by the gate and climb gently to the right to another stile with white markings. Ascend through the young trees to a stile giving access to a fire break and turn right up this to reach the road.

A few yards to the right, along the road past the windmill, turn off left onto the signposted footpath and, keeping to the fence on the left, start to drop down towards Turville which comes suddenly into view. Crossing stiles in the same direction join a short track into the village, almost opposite the church. (See Walk 26 for a history of Turville.)

Take the road almost opposite, past Sleepy Cottage to Square Close Cottages at the end of which a signposted bridleway continues on between hedges. Entering a field keep to the right at a Y-junction to climb the rounded ridge, passing the edge of a wood before running along the crest. Stiles lead through a small field to a road and turn left along the road leading past the entrance to Turville Court.

At the junction with the main road climb the bank on the right and follow a footpath across the field slightly to the left. At the hedge turn left and follow it to a stile and then continue along the other side towards Turville Grange, a delightful Georgian brick house. Keeping in the same field turn right just before the house and go past the ha ha to a beech tree at a corner. Then continue straight across the field ahead. In the distance across the valley Ibstone Church can be seen and on the same ridge, some way to the right, the windmill above Turville.

Over the stile into a mixed wood a distinct path drops, occasionally steeply, to a stile at the bottom. Cross the field by the wire fence to the stile and road. The head of the Turville valley is pleasantly green being surrounded by trees on all slopes. A few metres up the private road opposite, turn right onto a signposted bridleway through the woodlands. Where the main bridleway turns away sharply to the left continue straight on, along a narrower footpath. Cross the concrete drive which leads to farm barns and follow a narrowly defined footpath, marked by occasional white arrows, to a stile and field. Turning left ascend the field and, crossing a stile, keep to the right-hand side of the field before traversing next to the tree line above a side valley. Cross the stile by a concrete trough and ascend through the woods, crossing a track. The path turns left adjacent to the graveyard of Ibstone Church.

St Nicholas Church, Ibstone is worth a brief visit. Framed between a massive yew and a sycamore tree the church lacks formal architectural beauty but possesses immense charm with its squat wooden bell tower. Much of the building was built during the Norman period and still retains

Bottom of valley from Ibstone

some early twelfth-century carving above the door. Once the centre of the village, with the drifting of the settlement it became somewhat remote from it and consequently attempts were made to build a new church nearer to the new village centre. All attempts were frustrated though. The blame for failure was put upon the Devil and gave rise to the name of Hell Corner.

Continuing along the path, past the western side of the churchyard, keep to the main path past a couple of junctions and follow it when it drops steeply down to the left. At the bottom, which is a carpet of bluebells in season, turn left just past a wire fence and climb straight up to join a metalled drive, then turning right, pass the wooden Ibstone Cottage. This is the area which frustrated church builders and became known as Hell Corner. Go to the left up a gravel track, signposted as a bridleway and to Farside Cottage. Past the cottage keep on the track to the right through trees and bushes to the corner of the common. Follow the track to the right across the common or the bridleway around the left-hand edge of the common back to the start.

WALK 26
Fingest - Skirmett - Turville
(9km, 5³/₄ miles)

MAPS: O.S. 1:25,000 Pathfinder Sheets 1137 and 1156
O.S. 1:50,000 Landranger Sheet 175
Chiltern Society Footpath Map No. 11

Set at the head of the Hambleden valley where it splits into smaller tributaries this troika of villages epitomises the heart of the Chilterns. The names of all three villages are of Scandinavian origin from the period of the Danelaw, when King Alfred confined the invading Danes to eastern England. Despite this common history each village now has its own individual character and charm. Fingest is dominated by the church with its imposing tower, Turville has a cosy cluster of cottages around its tiny green, and Skirmett the brick houses along its single road. Climbing the ridges between each village the walk also offers some wonderful views, as well as exercise.

START (777,912): Fingest church, there is limited parking on the road. Fingest is best reached by turning off the B482 Marlow to Stokenchurch road at Bolter end or off the A4155 Marlow to Henley road at Mill End and following the Hambleden Valley. If parking is difficult it is possible to start the walk at Skirmett or Turville.

PUBLIC TRANSPORT: None.

ROUTE: *St Bartholomew Church, Fingest almost appears comical with its disproportionately large tower, yet both the tower and the narrower nave date from the Norman period. This unusual appearance is added to by the later addition of a twin gabled roof to the tower. The inside of the church has a simple austere charm reflecting the tower.*
From the church go left, past the Chequers Inn, along the road to the eastern end of the village and a signposted track off to the right. Passing the last farm note the granary barn resting upon

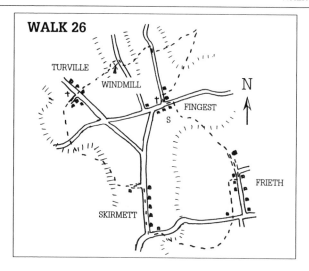

staddles. Follow the track, up the right hand side of the field, bending left into the next field below the treeline. Climb to the top edge of the field, where there is a seat to rest and contemplate the view back down to Fingest and the windmill on the ridge beyond. Pass through the gate at the top, marked with a yellow arrow, and follow a good footpath through beech woods to a field on the crest of the hill. Cross the field diagonally to the left to a new metal gate and into the woods again. Keep to the main track as it traverses around the top of the valley, running close to a wall for some distance and past the entrance to Frieth Court.

Joining a metalled road, continue straight on for a short distance to a signposted footpath through a gate just past the brick and flint cottage imaginatively called The Cottage. The path leads down the side of the cottage and past the door of Creighton Cottage (with a rope to protect the small garden) to a stile. Then turn left, between the hedge and a wire fence, and follow this traverse overlooking the valley to a stile and a minor road by Whitefield Cottage.

Cross the road and stile opposite and the turn diagonally right, into the right hand field, and descend just to the left of the remains of an old field boundary, now little more than a small weed covered

Fingest Church

bank, down towards the woods. Over the stile into the woods a good path leads, initially to the right and downwards, through the trees before passing old excavations and levelling off through mixed woods to a stile as part of a metal gate at the end of the woods. Turn right at the junction onto a bridleway which descends the ridge between hedgerows. At the road turn left towards Skirmett and then right at the road junction towards Fingest following the road through the strip of buildings, including the Old Crown and The Kings Arms pubs, which form the village of Skirmett.

Towards the far end of the village look for a public footpath signposted up the farm track opposite Meadowbrook. Follow this private drive, passing two more off to the left, to the top where the footpath continues over a stile straight ahead. Climb up between the fences and then go right along the bottom edge of woods from which viewpoint it is possible to trace much of the walk. The path bends left to climb into the woods before turning right again, by

Across the top of the Stonor Valley (walk 27)
The ruined St James's Church, Bix Bottom (walk 30)

Temple Island, River Thames near Fawley Court (walk 32)
Grey's Court from the Great Tower (walk 33)

vermin control signs, to traverse through the woods. Past a couple of fallen trees the path starts to descend becoming much steeper after a sharp right turn, marked by arrows, down to a stile. Cross the small field to more trees with a path leading through these to a gas pumping station and a drive down to the road. Across the road go diagonally right, through the field on a usually well trodden path, keeping right when joining another path to reach the edge of the field. Follow the path through the hedge and between hedgerows to join a road leading down to the centre of Turville.

Turville is a wonderful jumble of timber, brick and flint. As late as 1925 the main occupation was turning chair legs and rails for the factories in High Wycombe. Indeed time still seems to move slowly here but, as Jean Archer in her Hidden Buckinghamshire *recounts, for one resident last century the term "sleepy village" took on a new meaning. A girl went into convulsions and then into a sleep for nearly a decade, during which time her mother and sister spoonfed her on port and sugar. At the age of 21 she awoke still a child and presumably with a colossal hangover.*

St Mary's Church, in contrast to Fingest, has a very short squat tower dating from the fifteenth century. Inside, the church is very charming being partly Norman but mostly fourteenth century, with a memorial to William Perry who built Turville Park. Complementing the historic decorations is the recent addition of a beautiful stained glass-window designed by the local artist John Piper, set into a blocked-off Norman doorway. A more gruesome relic in the church is a stone coffin which, when opened, was found to contain a couple of burials. The later skeleton was of a woman with a hole in her skull giving rise to suggestions she was the victim of a hidden murder. In the graveyard itself are some good examples of bedboards or wooden grave markers which can occasionally be found in Chiltern graveyards. The Bull and Butcher nearby owes its existence to earlier restorations when, in the seventeenth century, masons working upon the church downed tools until refreshments were provided, so a local resident applied for a licence.

Opposite the small triangle at the centre of Turville a footpath is signposted up the track by the Old Schoolhouse to a stile. Continue straight up the hill over the stiles of a double fence, and climbing beside a fence, which bends left and then right at the top, to go round the windmill to the road at the top. The twelve-sided smock-mill, standing like a lighthouse overlooking the valley, has been converted into a private residence. Turn right along the road to the footpath signposted off to the left before the "10% slope" road sign. Follow the cutting down through the woods to a wire fence, where over a stile to the left, the path continues down through the trees to a stile. Go diagonally right to the gate at the corner of the field and a track which leads to the road.

Turn right along the road to a footpath which is signposted through the hedge on the left and then climb straight up to the trees. Before entering the woods there is a good view of Fingest and Skirmett in one direction and the white building of Ibstone House in the other. Yellow posts and arrows mark the route through the woods, turning right at the green gate to Hanger Estate to reach a T-junction. Turn right here, along a grassy path, over the crest of the hill continuing to follow the yellow marks. At the exit of the woods there is an excellent view of Fingest. The path drops straight down, between a hedge and wire fence, to a stile and then straight on, by a fence, to another stile and beside a garden fence to the road and Fingest village.

WALK 27
Turville Heath - Stonor
(9.6km, 6 miles)

MAPS: O.S. 1:25,000 Pathfinder Sheets 1137 and 1156
O.S. 1:50,000 Landranger Sheet 175
Chiltern Society Footpath Map No. 9

This walk offers some typically charming Chiltern views, whilst crossing the open valley between the high ground of Turville Heath and the hamlet of Pishill, before entering the equally typical beech woods. Dropping down again to the village of Stonor, the walk then climbs up through the grounds of Stonor Park overlooking the attractive house tucked away in a quiet side valley. On the high ground again the walk passes some pleasant views towards the windmill above Turville before returning to the start.

START (745,909): Turville Heath at the junction of the roads from Stonor and Turville. Parking a little up gravel road opposite signposted as a bridleway.

PUBLIC TRANSPORT: None

ROUTE: Turn right along the road to a shelter and follow the gravel drive signposted to Saviours opposite. Before the gateway to Saviours turn off left and through a small iron gate, to go along past a beech tree and beside the lawns of this converted church to a stile. Continue past a solitary tree to another stile and going straight on pass a group of trees in a hollow to reach an old iron kissing gate and a bridleway.

Turning right this bridleway leads along the crest of a ridge and into a field, following its edge to a stile and a sudden vista down the Stonor valley. Descend by the edge of the next field to a group of trees. Cut right, to a stile between two trees, before dropping down steeply between fields to the bottom of a valley. Cross the bridleway track, at the bottom, and go straight on up by the bank, at the edge

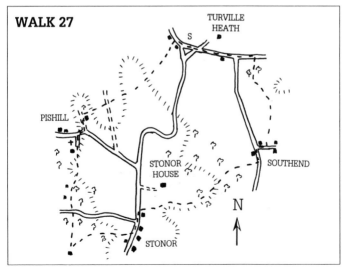

of the left-hand field ahead, to the top and a narrow road. Along the left-hand edge of the field over the road drop down to a stile in the corner. Continue on past some young conifers, then beside fence to a stile and turn left along a track the few metres to reach a junction with a road.

Turn right, the short distance to a road off to the left, signposted to Pishill Church and as the Oxfordshire Way. *Pishill actually means "the hill where peas are grown", although in 1811 a character called Wiggins was sent to court for "making a privey near the churchyard".* Up past the flint church, with its small wooden tower, at the end of the road follow the path to the left of the drive to Chapelwells and then shortly, at the Y-junction at the end of a wooden fence, take the left fork signposted PS17. Along the left-hand edge of a field cross a valley to a track and across this follow the steeply climbing path, up through tall spindly beech trees, to near a field on the right at the top. Keep straight on path marked PS17, at a junction with a path joining from the left, to reach another junction by some yew trees. Again keep straight on, this time marked OW, in the woods and below gardens of Maidensgrove to a road.

Across the road follow the path straight ahead, marked by white arrows (not the track to its left). At the junction near the end of the trees continue straight on, into a field and ahead towards the end of the hedge opposite. At the corner of the field near Lodge Farm go back and left across the field again to a stile into the wood. Follow the path ahead down a broad ridge to a stile into a field looking across to Stonor House. Continue straight on, down the ridge past a clump of trees, to cross a stile and then on to another by a yew tree and between gardens to the road in the village of Stonor.

Turn left and go past the road junction to the end of the village. Go through the tall kissing gate, on the right at the start of the metal fence, and climb towards a few trees, a little to the left of the ridge. White arrows mark the path, which levels off along the valley side facing Stonor House.

Despite the façade of mellow brick and Georgian windows Stonor House is essentially a Tudor E-shaped mansion but with parts, including the adjoining flint chapel, dating back as far as around 1280. Throughout this time it has remained the home of the Stonor family (now Lord Camoys), who initially made their fortune from sheep and wool which was sent by

Stonor House

barge from Henley down to London. However at the Reformation the Stonors were recusants, maintaining their Catholic beliefs and refusing to take the Oath of Supremacy which made the English monarch the the head of the church. Continuing to celebrate Mass in the chapel, one of only three in the country to boast uninterrupted worship, the family's fortunes consequently suffered as they were frequently fined and penalised. The family also took to hiding priests from the authorities and in particular the Jesuit Edmund Campion who managed to publish a book from a secret room in the roof before being caught and martyred. Only much later did the family's fortunes improve sufficiently for any improvements to the house, hence the Georgian windows, and indeed it wasn't until the Catholic Emancipation Act of 1829 that any of the family were able to hold public office again.

Straight on, the path leads into hawthorn trees and up to a gate in the deer fence and pine woods. The path is joined by a track to climb along the valley floor. At the top keep straight on, as more tracks join, to reach a road by the ornate flint and brick houses.

Turn left, to the junction, and then right, on the concrete road by the edge of the common of Southend. *The private house on the corner was formerly The Drovers pub, another reminder of the sheep farming that flourished here.* Before the end of the common and houses cross the stile, in the hedge on the left, and going along beside a fence pass the solitary tree. The windmill above Turville can be seen away to the right. Over the stile at the end cross the corner of the field, above a steep valley, to another stile into woods. Veer right and follow the white arrows, marking a path meandering through trees. Through a breach in a small mossy bank enter common woodland where a bridleway bends right leading through the bracken to a road. Turn left along the road and continue past a junction to the start.

WALK 28
Hambleden Valley
(10km, 6¼ miles)

MAPS: O.S. 1:25,000 Pathfinder Sheet 1156
O.S. 1:50,000 Landranger Sheet 175
Chiltern Society Footpath Map No. 11

The Hambleden Valley is one of the most charming, and at times popular, places in the Chilterns. Straight and broad it leads from a picturesque mill on the River Thames, past the historic and quaint village of Hambleden, and on to Skirmett whence it divides with arms going to Turville and Fingest. Occasionally the Hamble Brook flows along the valley and thus it's no surprise that this was one of the Chiltern valleys chosen by the Romans as the site for a villa.

This walk starts from Hambleden village, following the valley and meadows past hamlets to the edge of Skirmett. It then climbs to the east and the gently undulating arable land on top. Some road walking is involved in this section but don't be discouraged as it is usually quiet and quite pleasant.

START (785,866): Free car park signposted in Hambleden past the Stag and Huntsman pub. Hambleden is best reached from the south turning off the A4155 at Mill End.

PUBLIC TRANSPORT: None.

ROUTE: Return along the road, past the Stag and Huntsman, and on to the cross in front of the church.

By the small village green in the heart of the village the church of St Mary the Virgin with its much altered flint exterior almost appears too large for the village. Inside are a number of interesting items including: brasses, a fine Norman font, a charming monument with the alabaster figures of Sir Cope Doyley, his wife and ten children, and a nave altar constructed from a bedhead once used by Cardinal Wolsey.

Hambledon can also lay claim to being the birthplace of a couple of famous people. The first was Thomas de Canteloupe, born in 1218, who became Bishop of Hereford and renowned for fighting corruption and helping the poor as well as being an advisor to Edward I. Involved in a controversy, he was excommunicated and died in Italy en route to put his case to the Pope. Soon, however, miracles were occurring at his tomb in Hereford Cathedral, leading to his canonisation in 1320, the last Englishman to be made a saint until Edmund Campion this century. (Edmund Campion was also linked with the Chilterns, see Walk 27.) The second famous son of Hambleden was the Earl of Cardigan, infamous as the leader of the Charge of the Light Brigade.

In the graveyard are buried two other famous people, W.H.Smith, the founder of the newsagents' chain and Major George Howson, who was awarded

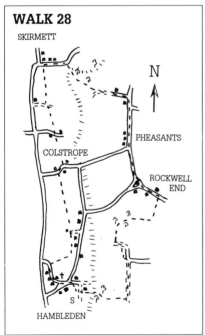

WALK 28

SKIRMETT

N

PHEASANTS

COLSTROPE

ROCKWELL
END

HAMBLEDEN

the Military Cross in the First World War and then went on to found the Poppy Factory at Richmond and the tradition of wearing poppies on Remembrance Day.

Take the road ahead, past a row of brick houses, and bend right beside the often dry and grassy bed of Hamble Brook, in front of the Old Bakery. Continue, beyond the end of the churchyard, to a kissing gate, by a hawthorn hedge, into the field on the right. Cross the field towards the houses and then bend a little left along the line of the valley to a kissing gate in the wire fence at the end of the field. Go on to another gate, and through a row of pine trees, to follow the hedge at the bottom of gardens to a gate and path ahead between more gardens. Cross the small road by Springfield and go straight on, by the hedge, to a gate into a field. Keep straight on and go through a kissing gate to a stile, and now with the hedge to the left, to kissing a gate at the end of the field. Continue straight on to another gate and a road.

Turn right and then left, through the attractive hamlet Colstrope Farm, but as road bends right, at Longspring House, take the bridleway signposted straight on along a track. This then passes between fields to reach another small road. Cross the stile ahead and go through the meadows on a path, aiming for the windmill at the top of the valley, to reach a track from the aptly named Flint Hall the other side of the valley. Continue by the hedge along the left-hand edge of the field ahead to a stile in the corner and then follow a row of sporadic hawthorn trees to a stile and the road at the edge of the village of Skirmett. (To the left then right, along the road, is the Old Crown pub.)

Turn right, up the road past cottages, to a left bend and a bridleway signposted off to the right in a strip of trees. This climbs out of the valley, along a ridge with some good views back down to the valley. Keep right at a Y-junction and go on up a path through bushes and young trees to join a track at the edge of the wood. Now onto the top the track leads past a flint house and becomes a small road.

At the junction turn right, past St Katherine's Convent, and then follow the road for quite some distance, passing a road off to the left and later, by the white cottages of Pheasants, one to the right to Colstrope. (The pub, marked on O.S. maps at Pheasants, no longer

Cottages in Hambleden village

exists.) Continue straight on to leave the main road to the left at a junction, by a farm where the main road bends right. Then go straight on, as a road joins from the right, and past the Rockwell End House farm shop to the end of sheds and trees on the right where there is a stile under a large oak.

Cross the field, parallel to the power cable posts, and when into the trees immediately turn right, along a path in a narrow band of trees. Entering a clearing, in a larger wood, keep to the main path, contouring left, to meet a track in older trees. This leads through more replanting and then on beside fields. Bend left joining another track leading towards farm buildings but before reaching them turn right, across a stile by a gate, and follow a fence to by-pass the farm.

Join the road ahead, to a junction of paths at the bend, and continue straight ahead, on the gravel track between fields. Gates either side of the track mark a junction. Turn right here, along the indistinct join of two fields and, beyond a solitary oak, cross the next field to the corner and a stile into trees. Join a track for a few metres but then fork right and down past stumps of felled trees, following occasional yellow arrows, to a clearer path in trees. The path then drops beside the fence of a field with excellent views down the valley to Mill End and the Georgian brick mansion of Culham Court across the River Thames. At the bottom go through the kissing gate, almost opposite across the track, and into playing fields. At the far right corner of the field is the car park and start. Whilst crossing both the seventeenth-century flint and brick Manor House and Kendricks, the old Rectory built for Rev Kendrick in 1724, can be seen.

WALK 29
Ewelme - Swyncombe
(10.8km, 6³/₄ miles)

MAPS: O.S. 1:25,000 Pathfinder Sheets 1137 and 1156
O.S. 1:50,000 Landranger Sheet 175
Chiltern Society Footpath Map No. 10

Ewelme lies at the bottom of the Chiltern scarp, not far from the River Thames. It is fitting therefore that Jerome K.Jerome, the author of the classic humorous book *Three Men in a Boat*, should be buried in the graveyard of this quiet and historical village. The walk joins the Ridgeway to flirt with the edge of the scarp and passes the Norman Swyncombe Church before returning to Ewelme via grassy lanes.

START (647,914): Ewelme Church which is easily reached on minor roads from Benson or Watlington. There is limited parking on the road near the church or more by the road junction past the church towards Swyncombe.

PUBLIC TRANSPORT: Occasional Chiltern Queen buses to Ewelme from Didcot and Wallingford (not Sundays).

ROUTE: *At the core of Ewelme a cluster of buildings, the church, almshouses, and a school, all date from the fifteenth century. Originally accompanied by a palace, which has disappeared, they owe their existence*

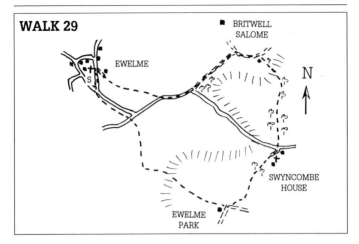

to Alice Chaucer, the grand-daughter of Geoffrey Chaucer, the poet. She inherited Ewelme from her mother's family. After a marriage to Thomas Montacute, Earl of Salisbury, who led the siege of Orleans in 1428 only to be killed by Joan of Arc's troops, she married again in 1430. This time it was to William de la Pole who became the Duke of Suffolk and a favourite of King Henry VI. Using their power and wealth they began building, often using techniques and styles more normally found in Suffolk. William came to a nasty end though for, after his role in the loss of France he was sent abroad in 1450 for safety, but didn't make it across the Channel, being seized and decapitated before being thrown overboard. Alice lived on for another 25 years in Ewelme.

It is apt that of the many memorials in St Mary's Church the tomb of Alice is the most outstanding. The beautifully carved figure of Alice lies on the tomb chest whilst below, in the dark, an emaciated figure in a shroud representing Alice in death can be seen.

From the west door of the church a passage leads down to the Almshouses, built around a cloister, and remarkably one of the earliest brick buildings in the Chilterns. Further down the slope is the school which is reputedly the oldest free Church of England school in the country and little altered on the exterior from when it was built.

From the church walk to the right along the road in the direction of Swyncombe for a short distance before turning off left up a track marked with a yellow arrow. Continue straight on, past the gate to a house, onto a greener track which in due course leads to a gate into a field and the first views of the Chiltern scarp. Keep in the same direction to cross the field to a stile and then veer slightly left to cross the next field. Over another stile continue in the same direction, with the Swyncombe valley ahead, dropping to the road.

Go to the left along the road until it bends right by the corner of a wood and turn left here onto the track, which follows the edge of the wood and is part of the Icknield Way. Beyond the wood keep straight on as a better used track joins from the left. Across the fields to the left is Britwell Salome House named after the thirteenth century lord of the manor Almaric de Sulehan, rather than after the Salome who danced for King Herod. Follow the track as it bends to the right and drops to a group of trees and the buildings of North Farm.

Turn right here, onto another track signposted as the Ridgeway footpath which passes to the left of the farm buildings before ascending a valley between a strip of trees to the left and a field to the right. The track curves right, round the top of the field, where it is worth a pause for the good view of Britwell Salome House, before climbing more steeply through woods up the scarp. At one point on the climb the path cuts through a bank, the remains of an ancient earthwork boundary. The woods on top have suffered storm damage and subsequent felling.

The path soon drops down the other side of the ridge. Keep straight on to follow the main track and, exiting the wood, cross the valley ahead by the right-hand side of the field. A stile by a gate gives access to the Cookley Green to Ewelme road opposite the road to Swyncombe Church. Follow the many signposts to the church past the handsome Georgian rectory built by Daniel Harris, a local man who combined the jobs of architect and Keeper of Oxford Gaol by using convicts as builders.

St Botolph Church, Swyncombe dates from the Norman period when the manor was held by Bec Abbey in Normandy. Unadorned by any tower its simple chancel and semi-circular apse are decorated by a herringbone pattern of flints. Although some of the windows are later additions and the interior has undergone some modifications it still retains the simple beauty created by the early builders.

From the church continue straight on along the path marked as the Ridgeway. This becomes an avenue lined with chestnut trees with the gardens and buildings of Swyncombe House to the left. Turn left over a stile, again signposted as the Ridgeway, and up the field to a stile and a wood. A good path leads straight up through the wood to emerge at the top of the Chiltern Scarp again. Keep to the left-hand side of a field, passing a footpath off to the left, and follow the curve to the right round the end of the field to a stile by the gate in the corner. A track leads to the buildings of Ewelme Park, passing between the breeze-block and brick and tile barns, to reach a cross-road of tracks. Ahead is the main house of the hamlet which is unfortunately only a grey replica of the Elizabethan house which stood here but which was destroyed by fire in 1913.

Turn right at the cross-roads to leave the Ridgeway taking a track which, within a short distance, finishes at the entrance to two fields. Enter the right-hand one and follow the hedge on the left. The descent gives good views of the valley ahead. Through the gate at the end follow the path along the valley bottom as it becomes a good track. At a cross-junction of tracks where the main track bends right continue straight on, up a slight climb, to a Y-junction. Turn right here to descend once again to the valley floor and follow the pleasant green track, called Grindon Lane, to the road.

Across the road a hole through the bushes leads to a gate into a field. There is no worn path in the field but follow the bottom of the dip before curving right to the far corner and gates to the road. A short distance along the Britwell Salome and Watlington road is Ewelme Church.

WALK 30
Nettlebed - Russell's Water
(10km, 6^1/$_4$ miles)

MAPS: O.S. 1:25,000 Pathfinder Sheet 1156
       O.S. 1:50,000 Landranger Sheet 175
       Chiltern Society Footpath Map Nos. 2 and 9

In his *Journeys of a German in England* Carl Philip Moritz described Nettlebed, in 1782, as 'a perfect village'. He had hurried here, on his walking tour, after an inhospitable reception in Henley-on-Thames. By contrast it took him three attempts before he was able to part from Nettlebed. Although perhaps not quiet as captivating as in his day Nettlebed still has considerable charm as well as the unusual preserved brick-kiln.

From Nettlebed this walk passes the smaller and quieter village of Crocker End before dropping down into the Bix valley. This valley must rank among the most attractive in the Chilterns and it's no surprise BBONT (Berks, Bucks, and Oxfordshire Naturalists' Trust) have a nature reserve there. The walk then climbs to the massive elevated Russell's Water Common before returning via another section of the Bix valley.

START (702,868): The T-junction of the A423 and B481, Watlington Street, in Nettlebed. There is limited parking near the entrance to Joyce Grove close to the junction or on The Old Kiln road.

PUBLIC TRANSPORT: Oxford Tube buses between Oxford and Victoria, London, via Henley, stop at the junction.

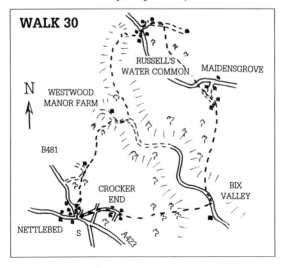

ROUTE: A few metres towards Henley from the junction a road forks off to the left to Crocker End and The Old Kiln, a residential road dominated by a conical brick kiln. *The combination of the Reading and London claybeds, found locally, and the abundance of wood for fuel led to Nettlebed becoming an early centre of tile and brick making. The earliest records date from 1365, whilst in 1416 Thomas Stonor used Nettlebed bricks in building Stonor house. The industry then flourished until the mid-nineteenth century. This preserved kiln, one of a least five that once stood locally, could hold 12000 bricks and, dating from the eighteenth century was working until 1938.*

Take the quiet Crocker End road, and past a junction, along to the long thin green of Crocker End. A footpath runs along its right-hand edge of the green. Continue, across roads, to the far end of the green and a track to the gate of The Leaze and the stile to its left. Follow the hedge by open parkland, with views of the brick and timber Soundess House, and round to the right above a deep little valley to cross the stile into a wood with yew plantation on the left. Keep to the main path past the unusual plantation of yews to join a track and continue along above the valley. Out of the trees the track descends by the edge of a couple of fields to the crumbling remains of St James's Church and road in a deep little valley. *Abandoned in 1875 the church was once the centre of Bix, but the village moved further south and a more recent church built there.*

Turn left along the road and then soon a track leading off to the right sloping up between hedges to enter the trees of the BBONT Warburg nature reserve. At the top keep straight on, as another track joins from the right, and along a crest with glimpses of the Stonor valley to the right. By a delightful brick cottage and Lodge Farm the track meets a road and follow this to where it bends right. Fork left, here, onto a gravel track leading to the large expanse of Russell's Water Common. *This vast common, unusually, grew in size even after the Enclosure Act, and as usual gives locals the right to gather firewood, hunt small game and graze pigs.*

Cross the road and go along the common over a slight crest. Beyond a track bend right to follow the grassy swath of common between trees. This leads across a valley and past telephone posts to a gravel road leading from a modern brick farmhouse. Turn left along this road through the bushes and trees of the common. Keep straight on at a junction (the Beehive Inn is to the right) and along beyond the pond of Russell's Water to the junction with the road. *The pond, the highest in the Chilterns, was due to natural clay on the chalk but has had to be relined from time to time.*

Turn left and later right past the converted old chapel, opposite the small green, and onto a track to the left of a house. Follow this bending right, at the gate to a field, and down between bushes to the valley bottom. Turn left along the valley which is the upper part of the Bix Valley. Follow the valley for some distance, eventually between wooden fences, to reach a T-junction. Turn right up a track, marked 28, to stiles either side, before Westwood Manor Farm, and cross the stile on the left.

A short climb leads to another track and, a little to the right, a stile into a wood. The grassy path climbs the crest of a ridge but then leaving the wood drop into a little valley and across to the top left corner of the field, with views back to Russell's Water Common. Across the stile keep beside the hedge, past a pond and modern house, to meet a track and turn left along this into beech woods. At a large right bend a footpath leads straight on, marked by white arrows in a slight valley. Fork left at a junction of several paths by an arrow on an oak tree, and then straight across at a junction by a large beech tree. Climb past old workings, more remains of the brick industry, to the top and bend left as other paths join. (If this route is missed keep on to the top and then along left by the scarp of old diggings.) Go along above the edge to join gravel track, from Nettlebed Reservoir, and follow this down, being joined by other tracks from the left, and past houses to the road. Turn left and go down past the Sun Inn back to the start.

WALK 31
Nuffield
(8km, 5 miles)

MAPS: O.S. 1:25,000 Pathfinder Sheet 1156
O.S. 1:50,000 Landranger Sheet 175
Chiltern Society Footpath Map No. 15

Situated on the edge of the Chiltern scarp, Nuffield overlooks Wallingford and the Thames Valley. From the charming church at the edge of the village this walk drops straight down the slope, following Grim's Ditch along some of its best preserved sections. The climb back up, although only a couple of hundred metres to the south, is a surprising contrast with sections of open fields and dense woods.

START (668,874): Nuffield Church is reached via minor roads off the A423 Wallingford to Henley-on-Thames road. There is limited parking by the church.

PUBLIC TRANSPORT: None.

ROUTE: *Holy Trinity Church, Nuffield is a delightfully simple church whose tower even lacks any pretensions of grandeur. The nave dates from the early twelfth century, with the north aisle and tower added a couple of centuries later. Indeed it is only the chancel, rebuilt in the mid-nineteenth century, that indicates that time has advanced beyond the fifteenth century. Inside the generally plain interior is the most elegantly shaped Norman, or possibly Saxon, font. The inscription on it has been variously translated but in essence exhorts the cleansing of the soul with the grace of God as well as baptism. On the floor, in front of the steps to the chancel, is a brass in memory of Benet English which has been dated around 1360. In the churchyard is buried William Morris, Lord Nuffield, who created much of the British motor industry and was the benefactor of a college in Oxford.*

A little down the road past a gate in a wall take the Ridgeway, signposted into a field on the left. Go along the top edge of the field,

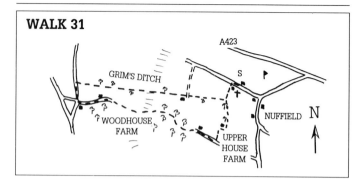

overlooking Wallingford and the Thames Valley, to a stile and then on, in a strip of trees, to a junction. Turn right, following the Ridgeway downhill in a band of beech trees and beside Grim's Ditch which the path soon crosses to be on the right.

Cross a farm drive via stiles to return to the left-hand side of the ditch. Continue down to a stile by a more broken section of the ditch and, across a little valley, climb up by the right-hand side of the ditch before later returning to the left-hand side at another stile. Keep along the path down to the bottom, where there is little sign of the ditch, and a short uphill climb into a wood and along the base of the now shallow ditch to emerge and follow a bank and row of conifers down to the road.

Turn left to a junction by a couple of houses and left again up the road towards Woodhouse Farm. Follow the road between the sheds of this farm, snug in its own valley, and up to bend right beside a wood. At a junction fork left and follow the track up the left-hand side of the field, with views to the left of the line of Grim's Ditch and back downhill towards Wallingford. This leads into a wood of pines and coppiced beech with a good path climbing steadily up. Go straight on, as a track joins from the left, to near the top and an area of replanting on the right. Keep left at a junction here and, into mature woods again, along a track leading past sheds and a dip to exit from the wood.

Past a house the track becomes metalled. At the end of the field, beneath power cables, turn left and along the edge of the field before bending right and across it, towards the white and timber house of

Upper House Farm. Turn right by the fence opposite and go along to a stile. Cross the drive and go along by the fence to turn left by a hedgerow. Follow the path between fences to a stile into woods and then to the right of a hollow to a metal ladder stile. Continue along the right-hand edge of the field and then into a strip of trees and over a stile to the top of Grim's Ditch and the Ridgeway. Straight ahead leads back to the start of the walk.

WALK 32
Henley-on-Thames - Fawley
(12.3km, 7 ³/₄ miles)

MAPS: O.S. 1:25,000 Pathfinder Sheet 1156
O.S. 1:50,000 Landranger Sheet 175
Chiltern Society Footpath Map No. 11

From the northern edge of Henley-on-Thames this walk follows beside Henley Reach, a straight section of the River Thames, famous as the site of the Royal Henley Regatta since 1839. The walk is best avoided during the Royal and Town regattas in July and early August due to the traffic congestion and crowds. Generally, on the river during summer, Mr Toads in motorboats are much more prevalent than Rattys but in the languid peace of an out-of-season day it is still possible to imagine Kenneth Graham's characters messing about in boats. Indeed the sylvan colour display of Great Wood seen on the climb away from the river, makes this walk particularly attractive in autumn.

Fawley, reached after a gentle ascent from the river, sits on a ridge overlooking the valley and feels like the top of the world. Its interesting village church chronicles, in monuments and mausoleums, the owners of the elegant Fawley Court passed earlier on the riverbank. Another ridge is followed in the descent back to Henley, past the Georgian Henley Park, and on through deer parkland.

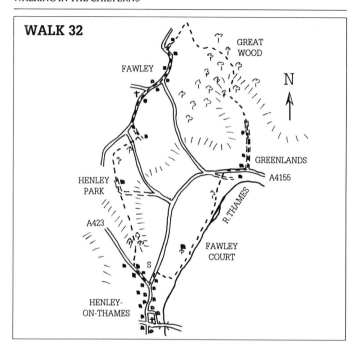

START (760,831): The junction of the A423 and A4155 roads at the northern end of Henley. There are parking spaces for a few cars on the A4155 beyond the yellow lines heading out of Henley, or various car parks within the town.

PUBLIC TRANSPORT: Henley is well served by train, bus and even boat services.

ROUTE: From the road junction go along the pavement of the A4155 towards Marlow, past a pair of toll houses. Shortly before a road sign indicating that it is 8 miles to Marlow turn right onto a wide path between railings and a wire fence. This leads past a first glimpse of Fawley Court at the head of an avenue of trees and then on down to the river. Turn left along the bank of Henley Reach, the section of the River Thames used for the Henley Regatta. On the opposite bank the large bow-windowed Remenham Court commands the scene, whilst back up the river Henley and its bridge can be seen.

Continue along the wide river bank until forced away from the river's edge by a strip of trees and a wire fence. Keep to the right-hand edge of what at first appears to be a grassy cul-de-sac to find two narrow footbridges separated by a flint and brick arch at the end. Cross the field ahead, parallel to the river, over which is situated the idyllic village of Remenham, to another footbridge crossing an ornamental canal leading to Fawley Court.

Fawley Court is an elegant brick house attributed by an inscription above a door to be tto he design of Christopher Wren, although Pevsner suggests it's more the work of James Wyatt with gardens by Capability Brown. Although closer to Henley than the village of Fawley this prime riverside site seems to have been the manorial site of the estate since it was granted to Herbrand de Sackville for his services in protecting the lands of Walter Gifford, one of William's followers, during the Norman Conquest. After passing between a number of families and being ransacked by the troops of Prince Rupert during the Civil War, the estate was bought in 1679 by William Freeman, a merchant from London involved in trade with the West Indies. He was responsible for the building of the present house which was later bought by the Mackenzies and resold again after the Second World War to the Marion Fathers, a Polish-Catholic organisation. The house is now open at certain times of the week.

Past the canal continue straight on through an overgrown field (beware of nettles in summer), parallel to a strip of trees on the riverbank, before rejoining the riverbank when the trees finish. Keep crossing footbridges and stiles until level with Temple Island in the river. The charming temple, created by James Wyatt, has a tremendous location looking up the length of Henley Reach to Henley itself. After another footbridge the path starts to ease itself away from the river which bends away towards Hambleden Lock. Two footbridges, joined by planks, lead through a strip of trees. The path continues in the same direction through parkland to another footbridge by a clump of trees and on again, crossing the driveway of Henley Management College, towards the white marks on a fence indicating the stile to the A4155 road.

Turn right along the pavement into Greenlands and where the pavement ends cross the road with extreme care (motorists are warned this is an accident blackspot). Go up Dairy Lane passing the odd little octagonal Keepers Cottage and further on a pair of brick semi-detached houses, to a broken gate with a sign Public Bridleway HA 37. Continue straight on up this track as it leads up the bottom of an open dry-valley surrounded by trees on the tops above. After the constant motion of the river the still peace of the valley, broken only by the call of pheasants, is a great contrast. As the valley begins to curve sinuously go straight ahead at a cross-junction of tracks and start to climb up from the valley floor. Great Wood, to the left, is one of the finest tapestries of tree textures to be seen in the Chilterns. Keep to the main track as it leaves the fields to contour along the valley side in open woodland.

After a distance the valley floor rises to meet the track at the point where there is a junction of tracks. Turn left off the track onto a wide footpath, signposted as Public Bridleway HA37. This climbs gently up the left-hand side of the beech covered valley to pass through cut channels near the top. These can become boggy at times but are easily by-passed to the side. Emerging onto the lip of the Thames valley the path, bound by hedgerows, passes between fields. A stile gives access to the field on the left which marks the end of the long climb up from the banks of the River Thames. Cross the field, heading towards the barns of Lower Woodend Farm, until forced to turn left along by the wire fence. After the enclosure of the valley and woods walking along this watershed feels like the top of the world. Cross the stile in the corner and go past the tastefully converted flint barns to a gate and the farm driveway. Turn left along the driveway to the road and turn left again.

Although the next section is along a road it is not without interest. At the first bend there is one of the most unusual houses in the Chilterns, the Round House. Built with cut stone, which is unusual for the area, it looks like a miniature castle turret with roof and windows all at odd angles. A little further on is the Walnut Tree, a pub and restaurant which does excellent food and has a children's play area.

The village of Fawley consists of sporadic houses with two centres, the first of which is the small village green, replete with a well, by a road junction. Continuing straight on, just past the road off to Fawley Bottom and the village pond, is the parish church of St Mary, the second centre. *The flint church, with its solid tower, has been much restored and altered over the years but it is the grounds which immediately attract attention with two striking mausoleums. Closest to the gate is the angular mausoleum of the Mackenzie's built in 1862, whilst nearer the tower is the earlier cupola topped Freeman's mausoleum. This was designed and built by John Freeman, an amateur architect, the nephew and heir of William Freeman who bought the estate. The succession of patrons has had its effect on the interior of the church as well with many alterations over the years, as befitting a living church. Two exceptional features from opposite ends of history are the Whitelocke monument, commemorating Sir James Whitelocke (died 1632), and a joyful stained glass window depicting the Tree of Life by John Piper, a local resident.*

Continuing the walk beyond the church, keep to the road passing a few houses and driveways to reach a right bend in the road by a chestnut tree. Turn off the road here onto a track signposted as a public footpath. Follow the track, past the gate to Homer House, and turn right off the track before reaching a field on the right and then pass to the right of the black corrugated metal shed. Continuing straight on, the path leads between wire fences to a road. Across the road climb the bank and immediately cross the low wooden rail on the right. Follow the left-hand edge of the field to a stile and continue up the edge of the next field to a broken stile. Crossing the driveway and stile follow the right-hand edge of the next field to reach a track.

Turn left along the track which marks the beginning of the descent along a ridge back into Henley. The track leads past a few houses and becomes tarmacked by the Georgian house of Henley Park. Passing through a gate the road immediately turns left but a kissing gate gives access to a farm track leading straight along the edge of a field. In the distance Medmenham can be seen downstream, along the Thames Valley. Beyond another kissing gate a path, worn into the grass, keeps fairly well to the crest of the ridge and begins to descend more steeply. A third kissing gate leads into woods and keeping straight on, pass a turning off to the left and round a few fallen trees to a T-junction at the edge of the woods. Turn right and downhill to cross a stile out of the woods and on, between a hedgerow and the wire fence of fields, to reach the A423 road. Turn left along the pavement back to the road junction at the start.

WALK 33
Henley-on-Thames - Rotherfield Greys
(10.7km, 6³/₄ miles)

MAPS: O.S. 1:25,000 Pathfinder Sheet 1156
O.S. 1:50,000 Landranger Sheet 175
Chiltern Society Footpath Map No. 2

Henley-on-Thames is undoubtedly the grandest town within the Chiltern. However for Carl Philip Morris, travelling in 1782, it proved too pretentious and unfriendly causing his hasty exit towards Nettlebed. Four years later Henley gained a new bridge, replacing an earlier one washed away by floods. Built by William Hayward and with the masks of Father Thames and Isis carved on the keystones, the bridge still remains one of the most elegant across the River Thames. Close to the bridge is a fifteenth-century chantry house as well as the church and almshouses.

From the town the walk follows a quiet valley up to the scattered settlement of Rotherfield Greys, visiting first the church with a splendid monument, then the village green, and finally the historic Grey's Court. The route works its way back to Henley-on-Thames passing through some majestic beech woods.

START (763,826): Henley-on-Thames by the bridge over the river or Market Place. There are several car parks within the town but these are often busy and expensive. An alternative to these is to try and find parking in Hop Gardens off the road to Rotherfield Greys by the entrance to Friar Park and start the walk here.

PUBLIC TRANSPORT: Henley-on-Thames is accessible by various forms of public transport.

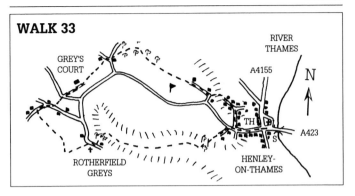

WALK 33

GREY'S COURT

RIVER THAMES

A4155

N

A423

TH

S

ROTHERFIELD GREYS

HENLEY-ON-THAMES

ROUTE: From the bridge over the River Thames go up the main street to the town hall at the top of Market Place. Continue up the road to its left, which becomes Gravel Hill, passing the Baptist church and some charming terraced houses. Hop Gardens joins from the right by the highly ornate gatehouse to Friar Park. Keep on climbing the main road passing Ancastle Green off to the left to just past the speed deregulation sign and turn left onto Pack And Prime Lane, in a cutting. Follow this quiet and soon un-made lane to past Westfield and then, before the barrier, leave it onto a footpath to the right of a tree. This leads between fences and hedges at the edge of an educational establishment before bending away and dropping down by trees all the way to the valley floor.

Cross the stile on the right at the bottom and go along by the fence following the wide valley base. At the end of the field cross the stile and pass to the right of a group of trees and on to a fence below the warm brick, tile and wood buildings of Lower Hernes. Over the stile ahead follow the track to a junction at the corner of a wood and then continue straight on, between two fields, along the bottom of the pleasantly curving valley dotted with groups of large trees. At the end of the fields, just as the track bends to the left to climb in an avenue of horse-chestnut trees, take a footpath to the right across a stile and then beside the fence on the left. Keep straight on, marked 38, at the junction at the next stile and ignore a stile and path in the fence on the left to cross the stile at the end of the field. The valley bends to the right and, just as part of Grey's Court at the head comes

153

into view, turn left over a stile marked 53 into the trees. A clear path leads up through the beech trees which float on a sea of bluebells in early summer. Over the stile at the top cross the field towards the church to a gate and the road.

St Nicholas Church, Rotherfield Greys, although greatly altered by Victorian restorers, does include some Norman architecture and there is evidence to suggest it has been the site of a church since Saxon times. With Grey's Court (passed later in the walk) in the parish the interior contains several memorials to past owners of the estate. In particular there is a fine brass of one of the original Knights of the Garter, Robert de Grey, dressed in armour and standing on a lion but even this is overshadowed by the Knollys Chapel. The exquisite monument is of Sir Francis Knollys (1514-1596) with his wife, Katherine shown reclining with a tiny baby. The base is flanked by rows of their many children whilst on the canopy are the larger kneeling figures of another son, the Earl of Banbury, and his wife who donated the monument and chapel. Katherine however actually lies in Westminster Abbey buried at the expense of Elizabeth I, who was a close cousin. Meanwhile the Earl of Banbury is thought to have been immortalised as the role model for Shakespeare's Malvolio in his Twelfth Night.

Two curiosities the church owns are a very early set of tithe measures and, among the papers, one by a rector who in 1823 grew an acre of poppies for high quality opium which he sold to the Society of Apothecaries Hall but which proved to be a commercial failure.

Turn right, along the road past the church, to the corner of the church wall (with The Malsters Arms to the right) and turn left along a signposted footpath to a stile. Go diagonally to the right across the field beneath power cables. The surrounding landscape appears very flat after the valley. Cross the stile into the next field and again go diagonally to the right to another stile and access to a bridleway between hedges. Turn right and follow the bridleway, which bends to the left and then climbs gently between hedges and fences to the road.

Go to the right along the road past a junction and bend right to the green-cum-cricket pitch of Greys Green. Skirt round this until between a large chestnut tree by the pavilion and a row of cottages a footpath is signposted along a grassy track. Keeping to the right along this leads to a stile, into trees through which a clear path drops to another stile at the bottom. Cross the field of the valley floor and climb up by a fence to a stile in the corner.

Across the small road a footpath ahead crosses another stile to join a private road. Keep straight on among varied trees, passing drives to Grey's Court (set back behind a ha-ha) to the entrance kiosk.

Grey's Court is a fascinating, if eclectic, group of buildings and gardens. The original owners since the Domesday Book were the de Grey family who gained favour fighting for Edward I in Wales and Edward III at Crecy, and who built a fortified manor of which several towers remain. The family died out at the Battle of Bosworth and the estates passed to the crown until Henry VII granted the estate to Robert Knollys, a court official. His son, Francis, became very important. Marrying a niece of Anne Boleyn he became Treasurer to Elizabeth I and for a time overseer of Mary Queen of Scots' captivity in Bolton. The Knollys used much of the stone from the earlier fortified manor to build the Tudor house which was later sold several times before being given to the National Trust in 1969. Within the grounds are a donkey wheel operated well which was used until 1914, a giant wisteria garden, and a maze laid out in 1980. Usually open afternoons, except Thursdays and Sundays, between April and September the grounds are well worth the entrance fee.

From the kiosk follow the left-hand side of the field, used as a car park, to a stile and on along a grassy track by a ditch and a row of pine trees. Over a stile climb the track to cross a footbridge over an improbably situated pond. Continue to pass a junction with a path off to the left and then a few metres ahead cross the stile on the left, near some farm sheds, and turn right by the fence to reach a small road.

Turn right along the road to a junction where, to the left of Broadplat Croft, a footpath is signposted to Assendon diagonally into the woods. Follow this footpath, marked with yellow arrows, through the majestic beeches. Keep to the main path to cross an unmarked path by the corner of a field. Continue on past holly bushes to a marked cross-junction by a shallow ditch and turn right, marked 48, to follow its edge. The path drops into the ditch and bends right passing one junction to reach another at the edge of the wood. Turn left onto a marked path following close to the edge of the wood. There is soon a stile to the right which is ignored to follow the track leading to the left of a hollow and across a small valley.

This then goes on through an area of bluebells until, near farm sheds in the field on the right, it bends a little to the left and then right again to a path through undergrowth leading on out of the wood to the edge of Badgemore Park golf course.

Go straight on between the greens towards a line of pine trees ahead and follow these on the left and then by a line of beech trees where a track emerges. Keep straight on this track to reach a stile by a gate to a tarmac road and follow this road along the ridge with glimpses to the left of Henley Park ridge. At a right bend just past Croft Cottage (hidden behind a fence) turn left and down on a footpath bending round to the right at the bottom before turning left by a garden fence to a road in a housing estate. Turn right to a junction with Hop Gardens on the right and take this road to its end by the gate house to Friar Park and turn left back down to Henley and the start.

WALK 34
Checkendon - Ipsden - Stoke Row
(13.7km, 8¹/₂ miles)

MAPS: O.S. 1:25,000 Pathfinder Sheet 1156
O.S. 1:50,000 Landranger Sheet 175
Chiltern Society Footpath Map No. 15

From Checkendon Church, opposite a row of timbered cottages, this walk passes through some attractive woodland before dropping down the scarp to the village of Ipsden, a short distance from the River Thames. One of the two wells in the Chilterns donated by Indian Rajas in the mid-nineteenth century is in the village, whilst the other more famous Maharajah's Well is visited later on the walk at Stoke Row. A large proportion of the walk is on tracks or quiet roads making a change from the other walks in this book.

START (664,830): Checkendon Church, most easily approached on the minor road to Checkendon off the A4074. Limited parking but

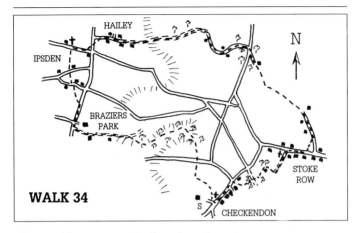

other parking spots can be found nearby.

PUBLIC TRANSPORT: Chiltern Queens bus service from Reading (not Sundays).

ROUTE: *With its chancel and semi-circular apse the church of St Peter and St Paul, Checkendon, bears a striking resemblance to the church at nearby Swyncombe (Walk 29). Consequently it may have been built by the same monks from Bec in Normandy, but whereas the church at Swyncombe retained its early simplicity that at Checkendon has been altered and enlarged, particularly with the addition of a fourteenth-century tower. The interior has likewise been frequently altered although retaining many earlier features. Particularly worth noting are: the thirteenth-century mural painting of Christ and the Apostles, several fifteenth-century brasses including that of the grandly attired John Rede, and the modern engraved window, a memorial to Eric Kennington the artist and friend of Lawrence of Arabia.*

From the church take the footpath signposted along the drive of Checkendon Court, with its carefully manicured yews. At end of churchyard wall turn right on the path running beside railings. Keeping left at a junction follow the path beside the hedge of Checkendon Court, which allows just one glimpse through a metal gate to the house rebuilt in the Tudor style in 1920. Continue on,

The ornate Maharajah's Well, Stoke Row

between a paddock and a wood, leading straight into more woods, and to be joined from the left by another path. Bend right at the end of the wood and along its edge to a stile and then by a fence to a road.

Cross the stile opposite and go across the field to a stile near the corner of the wood ahead. A few white arrows mark a path through the beech trees slanting down into a valley. At the junction with tracks, at the bottom, take the track running down along the valley. Turn left where it meets another valley and track, again keeping to the valley bottom. At the bottom go straight on, at a junction of tracks and between coppiced beeches, until part way to the fields ahead look for an indistinct green path climbing from another coppiced beech on the right. This soon becomes a bit more distinct climbing near the left-hand edge of the wood, overlooking The Bottomfarm House. Continue past a junction, beside the remains of a fence, to meet a track at the top.

Turn left along the track, gently descending with glimpses of the Thames Valley. Continue, past some cottages, down to the bottom and a short climb near the Gothic Braziers Park to a road junction. Turn right, continuing on towards Ipsden at a second junction. At the start of the next field on the left take the footpath signposted across it heading towards the school in the scattered Ipsden settlement. Turn left along the road to the end of the beech hedge by the school and then right along a track past a small pavilion and straight on into a row of trees. *A diversion down the road and back again can be made to the gates of Ipsden House. This has been the home of the Reade (or Rede) family since the times of Henry the VIII and was once described as "the coldest house in Europe" by Charles Reade, the novelist, famous in Victorian times for melodramatic works such as* The Cloister and the Hearth. Continue past a mock stone circle and then beside the right-hand edge of a field overlooking Ipsden and down to another road.

Straight across climb the bridleway, beside the flint garden wall of a Georgian house, and go straight on at the top past the Celtic-cross war memorial commemorating the fourteen dead and fifty-two others who served in the First World War from this small community. Continue to the road and church opposite. *The small thirteenth-century church has great rustic charm. It also possesses an early example of recycling as the brass of Thomas Englysche (1525) apparently has the figure of a lady from a hundred years earlier on the other side. Beside the entrance to the churchyard is the cast-iron well head presented by the Indian Rajah Sir Deonarayun Sing KSI in 1865, a year after the more famous well at Stoke Row. The well was working until the 1950s.*

Turn right, along the straight road, but before the junction cross a stile on the left and go across the corner of the field. Continue over another road and the corner of the field beyond to reach the road towards Hailey. Go to the right along this, keeping straight on through the hamlet and past the King William IV pub overlooking the valley and Wellplace. Past Hill Barn continue on climbing up the track which has good views back over the valley. Keep straight through beech trees, as another track joins from the left, at the top and then bend left, beside the wire fence of private woods, at a Y-junction. Follow the track, with glimpses down to valley on right, which becomes metalled after the drive to Fludger's Wood and continue along the road for some distance, passing a few farms, to a road T-junction.

Over the road a track leads off to the right (not the footpath signposted to the left). Follow this through trees and then straight on, beside a fence, past the entrance to sheds. This bridleway then leads between hedges for some distance eventually to join a road from Stoke Row Farm. Keep straight on along the road up to and just past the drive to The Pond House where there is a footpath off to the right between hedges. This leads to the main road through Stoke Row along which turn right.

The Maharajah's Well, under an ornate dome, is set back from the road here. Its existence is the result of a conversation between Edward Anderdon Reade, elder brother of Charles and Lieutenant-Governor of the North Western Provinces, and the Maharajah of Benares about the lack of water in Stoke Row and the beatings children got for drinking without permission. Sometime later as a gift to England and E.A.Reade the Maharajah paid for the well to be dug to provide the residents of Stoke Row with free water. This proved quite a task as the depth of 368ft, marginally greater than the height of St Paul's Cathedral, had to be dug by hand. However in 1864 the well opened, the exotic dome making it look grand in the pictures sent to the Maharajah. Maintenance of the well was initially paid for by the sale of cherries from a four-acre orchard, on the other side of the footpath, also donated by the Maharajah. The well was used until 1939 but continues to be maintained by the Maharajah's Well Trust.

Turn left along School Lane, past the church, and on until it becomes an un-made track. Maps show a path diagonally across the field on the right, however, at the end of the field a sign indicates to Checkendon between the wire fences of fields then turning left into woods. Keep left shortly at a Y-junction and, past sheds, along by a strip of beech trees a path leads into more woods. Bending right and down by the wire fence leads to a bridleway at the valley bottom.

Straight across a footpath climbs near the edge of trees and round, across a gap in the trees, above a cottage. Then go left up through more trees parallel to the gap to reach a stile into a field. Cross by the poles to a stile on the right in the corner and over this go down by edge of the next field to the trees again. Keep to the left, to a stile in a few metres, and along between fences to join a drive and then on to meet the road. Turn left, following the main road past a junction back to Checkendon Church.

WALK 35
Goring - Whitchurch
(12.5km, 7 ³/₄ miles)

MAPS: O.S. 1:25,000 Pathfinder Sheets 1156, 1172, 1155*, 1171*
O.S. 1:50,000 Landranger Sheets 174* and 175
(* only for very short distance)
Chiltern Society Footpath Map No. 16

Goring, linked with the village of Streatley on the other side, is one of the old crossing points of the River Thames. Between Goring and Whitchurch, the next crossing place downstream, is the Goring Gap. This marks the southern boundary of the Chilterns where the River Thames has cut through the chalk between the Chilterns and the Berkshire Downs. This walk follows the Thames on its course through the gap and between the two villages. Leaving the river the walk returns over the top of the chalk through a mixture of open farmland and woodland.

START (600,807): There are a couple of car parking areas signposted in Goring.

PUBLIC TRANSPORT: Goring is on the Thames Line rail route, between Reading and Oxford.

ROUTE: Follow the main street down through Goring towards the

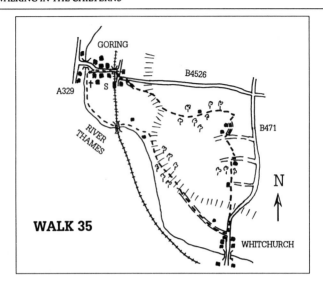

GORING

B4526

A329

S

RIVER
THAMES

B471

N

WALK 35

WHITCHURCH

bridge and Streatley. Take the little road on the left before the bridge, which leads past Goring Mill Gifts, and over the mill race to the river. *Although the Icknield Way crossed the river nearby there was no bridge until as late as 1838. Before then crossings were made by ferry or fording, a sometimes perilous operation as in 1674 when fifty people were drowned.*

Turn left to follow the riverbank, downstream away from the lock and weirs. Shortly the church of St Thomas, which has substantial Norman remains of a former nunnery, can be glimpsed to the left but is only accessible by a diversion before the bridge. Continue along the river bank for quite a while, passing a number of sadly neglected boathouses and then into open fields. As the river begins to meander to the left, it also braids, creating a number of small islands, one of which is all but completely occupied by a defensive pillbox. Continuing downstream, Grove Park stands in splendour, on the other bank, with terraced lawns down to the river. Across a stile go under the busy railway bridge, carrying the main line to Oxford over the river. Keep along the river bank, through a gate, until reaching Ferry Cottage where the path turns left over a small footbridge and then goes straight on, past horse paddocks, to a T-junction with a bridleway.

Turn right, along this bridleway, contouring just above the river flood plain. Keep to the bridleway and enter a mixed wood with a high proportion of yew trees, whose roots just about prevent the steep valley side from forming a scree slope. A path down to the right at one point leads to another pillbox which is open. The bridleway then starts a long climb to the top of the valley side, with glimpses across the valley to the grand eighteenth-century Basildon Park, built by John Carr of York and now a National Trust property. At the top of the climb the trees have suffered considerable wind damage but the route is well marked and a wire fence keeps the unsuspecting walker away from a surprisingly large cliff.

The bridleway continues, leading out of the woods, to cross the crest of a ridge between hedges and then across a valley to steps up to a farm road. Continue straight on along the farm road, past several farm cottages and above the grounds of Coombe Park, to reach the B471 road near the edge of the village of Whitchurch. *Whitchurch is a pleasant old-world place with a Victorian toll bridge across the River Thames which is worth a visit if time allows.*

Cross the road and turn left up a footpath above the road to re-cross the road to the Whitchurch War Memorial. Continue by the road for a few metres to a footpath, signposted to Coombe End, leading straight on as the road bends to the right. Over the stile, marked GH27, near power posts follow the left-hand edge of the field onto the plateau above the valley. Pass through a kissing gate, with views of the village of Whitchurch Hill away to the right, and along the green track. The footpath is signposted around to the right of Beech Farm and then, keeping to the same direction, go along the left-hand edge of the field beyond the drive to the woods. A clear footpath leads through the trees bending left to a faint cross-junction where daylight can be seen ahead. Turn right, away from a "Private, Danger" sign, and go along a small path marked with occasional yellow splodges on the trees. This then leads between wire fences and beneath power cables before going through a few more trees to join a drive. Keeping to a similar direction pass a barn and follow the drive, beside a row of chestnut trees, to a gate and road.

Turn right, along the road to Pine Paddock, and then turn left, through the gate opposite, and go diagonally to the left across the field to a stile. Pass the group of trees in the next field to a stile near a tiled roofed cottage. Turn right, along the road to a junction, and turn left here along the road past Spring Cottage and others. The road bends left above a steep little valley to Lavender Cottage where a footpath drops down to the right in the edge of trees.

Turn left along the track at the bottom, down a suddenly secluded and wooded valley. Through the gate of Bottom Farm House, continue to the end of the drive and then go straight on beside a fence to a gate and on down along the bottom of the valley to a gate into woods. Continue down, eventually bending left a little to reach a junction. Cross the track, which leads to an area of replanting, and climb the path beside a wire fence and later in a trough to a gate and a junction. Turn right along the track for a few metres to another junction and fork right. Keep to the marked track which crosses a forest road and later, by another area of replanting, descends down a slight valley to a stile at the edge of the trees.

Go straight on through bushes to another stile and then climb up along the right-hand edge of a field. Follow the edge round to the left at the top and along to a stile in the corner of the field, with views down to the river. Keep straight on along the top edge of the next field which descends, at the end, to a stile into playing fields on the right. Go diagonally across these to a stile at the junction between conifer and hawthorn hedges. This leads to a residential road which is followed to the left then right to meet the main road. Turn left to the junction by The Queens Arms and turning right then left cross the railway on the road towards Streatley. This road soon takes you back to the centre of Goring.

APPENDIX A
Other Chiltern Walks

A number of long distance walks pass through the Chilterns.

1. **The Ridgeway.** (145km, 90 miles) This is the classic long distance walk of the region. From Avebury in Wiltshire it follows the principles of the ancient Icknield Way along the top of the chalk to cross the River Thames at Goring. It then follows the edge of the scarp (or close to it) along the Chilterns to finish at Ivinghoe Beacon. It is well signposted.

2. **The Oxfordshire Way.** (104km, 65 miles) Links the Cotswolds with the Chilterns, running from Bourton-on-the-Water to enter the Chilterns near Watlington and finish at Henley-on-Thames. It is reasonably well signposted.

3. **The North Buckinghamshire Way.** (48km, 30 miles) From Milton Keynes, where it links with the Grafton Way, this just enters the Chilterns to connect with the Ridgeway at Chequers Knap. It could easily be continued along the South Bucks Way. It is generally well signposted.

4. **The South Buckinghamshire Way.** (53km, 33 miles) Very much within the Chilterns this leaves the Ridgeway near Chequers and beyond Great Missenden follows the Misbourne valley to Denham Lock. Walk 11 covers some of the best sections. The South Bucks Way is generally well signposted.

5. **The Thames Walk.** (250km, 156 miles) From Putney to the source of the River Thames this walk has been devised by the Ramblers Association. It follows the river as closely as possible but ideally needs a few more bridges, replacing defunct ferries, to avoid detours. It is generally not signposted.

6. **The Chess Valley Walk.** (13km, 8 miles) Although relatively short this follows the entire length of the delightful River Chess from Pednormead End in Chesham to the River Colne near

Rickmansworth. Walk 15 covers much of the Chess Valley. The Chess Valley Walk is well signposted.

7. **The Beeches Way.** (26km, 16 miles) From the River Thames near Cookham to the Grand Union Canal at West Drayton. En route it crosses Burnham Beeches and Stoke Common (Walks 22 and 23). It is generally well signposted.

Buckinghamshire and Bedfordshire County Councils have both signposted a number of short circular walks (marked CW on signposts). Leaflets for these can be obtained at tourist information centres, Bucks walks also from the County Recreational Paths Officer.

A few other walking places:
Warburg Reserve Nature Trail. (720,878) Bix Bottom. Nature trail around the BBONT run nature reserve. An indication of the wealth of fauna and flora protected in the reserve is that fifteen species of orchids are found there.

Church Wood RSPB Nature Reserve. (973,873) Hedgerley, along track beside Hedgerley Court Farm. Marked walks in attractive mixed woodland with over eighty recorded species of birds.

Chiltern Sculpture Trail. (725,955) Cowleaze Wood on Stokenchurch to Christmas Common road. Marked trails passing modern sculptures set in a woodland environment.

Wendover Woods. (889,090) Halton Wood picnic site reached off the road to St Leonards. A number of trails have been laid out by the Forestry Commission as well as an orienteering course.

APPENDIX B
Places to Visit

A number of the stately houses mentioned in the guide are open to visitors. Normally these are closed during the winter months and only open for two or three afternoons per week in summer.

National Trust properties

Ashridge Monument:	044 285 227
Basildon Park:	0734 843040
Greys Court:	0491 628529
Hughenden Manor:	0494 532580
West Wycombe Park:	0494 524411

Other properties

Chenies Manor:	0494 762888
Fawley Court:	0491 574917
Stonor Park:	0491 638587
Chiltern Open Air Museum :	0494 871117

Situated at Newland Park, Chalfont St Giles. Among the Chiltern buildings relocated and preserved on this site are a collection of old barns, a forge, a furniture factory and the High Wycombe Toll house, complete with period interior.

APPENDIX C

Public Transport

With the deregulation and privatisation of bus services trying to find out about bus timetables can be quite a search. Hopefully these phone numbers will provide the answers.

Buckinghamshire Travel Line (Aylesbury)	0296 382000
Hertfordshire Travel Line (Watford)	0923 257405
Bedfordshire Travel Line	0234 228337

Buses

Aylesbury bus station:	0296 84919
Chiltern Queens:	0491 680354
Hemel Hempstead bus station:	0442 255619
High Wycombe bus station:	0494 520941
Luton Buses:	0582 404074
Oxford Tube:	0865 772250
Reading bus station:	0734 583747
Slough bus station:	0753 524144
Uxbridge bus station:	0895 236598
Watford bus station:	0923 229811

Trains (information bureau)

London (Paddington for Thames Valley Line to Goring):
071 262 6767
London (Marylebone for Chiltern Line to Wendover):
071 387 7070
For trains to Henley-on-Thames: 071 928 5100
London Underground: 071 222 1234

BIBLIOGRAPHY

The Chilterns can lay claim to a great number of authors: John Milton escaped there from the Great Plague; Frankenstein was completed when the Shellys lived in Marlow; Jerome K.Jerome, Kenneth Grahame, George Orwell, G.K.Chesterton, Roald Dahl, Graham Greene, Cowper, and Enid Blyton all at sometime lived in the area. Despite this there are few great books about the area offering more than facts and history. Perhaps the most evocative book remains *Chiltern Country* by H.J.Massingham which, published in 1940, captures the pre-war Chilterns.

Chequers, J.Gilbert Jenkins: Pergamon Press 1967
Chiltern Country, H.J.Massingham: Batsford, 1940
Chiltern Villages, V.Burden: Spur, 1972
Country Churches of the Chilterns, H.S.Rice: Corinthian, 1983
Companion into Buckinghamshire, M.Fraser: Methuen, 1950
Hidden Buckinghamshire, J.Archer: Countryside Books, 1989
Hidden Hertfordshire, J.W.Whitelaw: Countryside Books, 1988
Highways and Byways * (written at about the turn of the century)
Hilltop Villages of the Chilterns, David and Joan Hay: Phillimore and
    Co, 1971 (a history of Cholesbury and Hawridge)
Oxfordshire and Buckinghamshire Pubs, J.Camp: Batsford, 1965
Portrait of the Chilterns, E.Cull: Robert Hale, 1982
Shire County Guide *
The Buildings of England *, N.Pevsner: Penguin
The Chilterns, K.Fitzgerald: Batsford, 1972
The Chilterns and Thames Valley, S.E.Winbolt: G.Bell, 1932
The Dashwoods of West Wycombe, Sir Francis Dashwood: Aurum
    Press, 1987
The Icknield Way, A.Bulfield: T.Dalton, 1972
The King's England *, A.Mee: Hodder & Stoughton
The Living Land, M.Smith: Spur, 1973 (a natural history of the area)
The Victoria County Histories *
View of the Chilterns, B.J.Bailey: Robert Hale, 1979

* Buckinghamshire, Hertfordshire and Oxfordshire volumes.

NOTES

NOTES

NOTES

CICERONE GUIDES

Cicerone publish a wide range of reliable guides to walking and climbing in Britain,
and other general interest books.

LAKE DISTRICT - General Books
A DREAM OF EDEN
LAKELAND VILLAGES
LAKELAND TOWNS
REFLECTIONS ON THE LAKES
OUR CUMBRIA
THE HIGH FELLS OF LAKELAND
CONISTON COPPER A History
LAKELAND - A taste to remember (Recipes)
THE LOST RESORT?
CHRONICLES OF MILNTHORPE
LOST LANCASHIRE
THE PRIORY OF CARTMEL

LAKE DISTRICT - Guide Books
CASTLES IN CUMBRIA
THE CUMBRIA CYCLE WAY
WESTMORLAND HERITAGE WALK
IN SEARCH OF WESTMORLAND
CONISTON COPPER MINES Field Guide
SCRAMBLES IN THE LAKE DISTRICT
MORE SCRAMBLES IN THE LAKE DISTRICT
WINTER CLIMBS IN THE LAKE DISTRICT
WALKS IN SILVERDALE/ARNSIDE
BIRDS OF MORECAMBE BAY
THE EDEN WAY
WALKING ROUND THE LAKES

NORTHERN ENGLAND (outside the Lakes
BIRDWATCHING ON MERSEYSIDE
CANOEISTS GUIDE TO THE NORTH EAST
THE CLEVELAND WAY & MISSING LINK
THE DALES WAY
DOUGLAS VALLEY WAY
HADRIANS WALL Vol 1 The Wall Walk
HERITAGE TRAILS IN NW ENGLAND
THE ISLE OF MAN COASTAL PATH
THE LANCASTER CANAL
LAUGHS ALONG THE PENNINE WAY
A NORTHERN COAST-TO-COAST
NORTH YORK MOORS Walks
THE REIVERS WAY (Northumberland)
THE RIBBLE WAY
ROCK CLIMBS LANCASHIRE & NW
THE YORKSHIRE DALES A walker's guide
WALKING IN THE SOUTH PENNINES
WALKING IN THE NORTH PENNINES
WALKS IN THE YORKSHIRE DALES (3 VOL)
WALKS IN LANCASHIRE WITCH COUNTRY
WALKS TO YORKSHIRE WATERFALLS (2 vol)
WALKS ON THE WEST PENNINE MOORS
WALKING NORTHERN RAILWAYS EAST
WALKING NORTHERN RAILWAYS WEST

DERBYSHIRE & EAST MIDLANDS
WHITE PEAK WALKS - 2 Vols
HIGH PEAK WALKS
WHITE PEAK WAY
KINDER LOG

THE VIKING WAY
THE DEVIL'S MILL (Novel)
WHISTLING CLOUGH (Novel)
WALES & WEST MIDLANDS
THE RIDGES OF·SNOWDONIA
HILLWALKING IN SNOWDONIA
HILL WALKING IN WALES (2 Vols)
ASCENT OF SNOWDON
WELSH WINTER CLIMBS
SNOWDONIA WHITE WATER SEA & SURF
SCRAMBLES IN SNOWDONIA
SARN HELEN Walking Roman Road
ROCK CLIMBS IN WEST MIDLANDS
THE SHROPSHIRE HILLS A Walker's Guide
HEREFORD & THE WYE VALLEY A Walker's Guide
THE WYE VALLEY WALK

SOUTH & SOUTH WEST ENGLAND
COTSWOLD WAY
EXMOOR & THE QUANTOCKS
THE KENNET & AVON WALK
THE SOUTHERN-COAST-TO-COAST
SOUTH DOWNS WAY & DOWNS LINK
SOUTH WEST WAY - 2 Vol
WALKING IN THE CHILTERNS
WALKING ON DARTMOOR
WALKERS GUIDE TO DARTMOOR PUBS
WALKS IN KENT
THE WEALDWAY & VANGUARD WAY

SCOTLAND
THE BORDER COUNTRY - WALKERS GUIDE
SCRAMBLES IN LOCHABER
SCRAMBLES IN SKYE
THE ISLAND OF RHUM
CAIRNGORMS WINTER CLIMBS
THE CAIRNGORM GLENS (Mountainbike Guide)
THE ATHOLL GLENS (Mountainbike Guide)
WINTER CLIMBS BEN NEVIS & GLENCOE
SCOTTISH RAILWAY WALKS
TORRIDON A Walker's Guide
SKI TOURING IN SCOTLAND

REGIONAL BOOKS UK & IRELAND
THE MOUNTAINS OF ENGLAND & WALES
VOL 1 WALES
VOL 2 ENGLAND
THE MOUNTAINS OF IRELAND
THE ALTERNATIVE PENNINE WAY
THE RELATIVE HILLS OF BRITAIN
LIMESTONE - 100 BEST CLIMBS

*Also a full range of EUROPEAN and OVER-
SEAS guidebooks - walking, long distance
trails, scrambling, ice-climbing, rock climbing.*

---

*Other guides are constantly being added to the Cicerone List.
Available from bookshops, outdoor equipment shops or direct (send s.a.e. for price list) from
CICERONE, 2 POLICE SQUARE, MILNTHORPE, CUMBRIA, LA7 7PY*

CICERONE GUIDES

Cicerone publish a wide range of reliable guides to walking and climbing abroad

FRANCE
TOUR OF MONT BLANC
CHAMONIX MONT BLANC - A Walking Guide
TOUR OF THE OISANS: GR54
WALKING THE FRENCH ALPS: GR5
THE CORSICAN HIGH LEVEL ROUTE: GR20
THE WAY OF ST JAMES: GR65
THE PYRENEAN TRAIL: GR10
THE RLS (Stevenson) TRAIL
TOUR OF THE QUEYRAS
ROCK CLIMBS IN THE VERDON
WALKS IN VOLCANO COUNTRY (Auvergne)
WALKING THE FRENCH GORGES (Provence)
FRENCH ROCK

FRANCE / SPAIN
WALKS AND CLIMBS IN THE PYRENEES
ROCK CLIMBS IN THE PYRENEES

SPAIN
WALKS & CLIMBS IN THE PICOS DE EUROPA
WALKING IN MALLORCA
BIRDWATCHING IN MALLORCA
COSTA BLANCA CLIMBS
ANDALUSIAN ROCK CLIMBS

FRANCE / SWITZERLAND
THE JURA - Walking the High Route and
  Winter Ski Traverses
CHAMONIX TO ZERMATT The Walker's Haute
Route

SWITZERLAND
WALKING IN THE BERNESE ALPS
CENTRAL SWITZERLAND
WALKS IN THE ENGADINE
WALKING IN TICINO
THE VALAIS - A Walking Guide
THE ALPINE PASS ROUTE

GERMANY / AUSTRIA
THE KALKALPEN TRAVERSE
KLETTERSTEIG - Scrambles
WALKING IN THE BLACK FOREST
MOUNTAIN WALKING IN AUSTRIA
WALKING IN THE SALZKAMMERGUT
KING LUDWIG WAY
HUT-TO-HUT IN THE STUBAI ALPS

ITALY & SLOVENIA
ALTA VIA - High Level Walkis in the Dolomites
VIA FERRATA - Scrambles in the Dolomites
ITALIAN ROCK - Rock Climbs in Northern Italy
CLASSIC CLIMBS IN THE DOLOMITES
WALKING IN THE DOLOMITES
THE JULIAN ALPS

MEDITERRANEAN COUNTRIES
THE MOUNTAINS OF GREECE
CRETE: Off the beaten track
TREKS & CLIMBS JORDAN
THE ATLAS MOUNTAINS
WALKS & CLIMBS IN THE ALA DAG (Turkey)

OTHER COUNTRIES
ADVENTURE TREKS - W. N. AMERICA
ADVENTURE TREKS - NEPAL
ANNAPURNA TREKKERS GUIDE
CLASSIC TRAMPS IN NEW ZEALAND
TREKKING IN THE CAUCACUSUS

GENERAL OUTDOOR BOOKS
THE HILL WALKERS MANUAL
FIRST AID FOR HILLWALKERS
MOUNTAIN WEATHER
MOUNTAINEERING LITERATURE
THE ADVENTURE ALTERNATIVE
MODERN ALPINE CLIMBING
ROPE TECHNIQUES IN MOUNTAINEERING
MODERN SNOW & ICE TECHNIQUES
LIMESTONE -100 BEST CLIMBS IN BRITAIN

CANOEING
SNOWDONIA WILD WATER, SEA & SURF
WILDWATER CANOEING
CANOEIST'S GUIDE TO THE NORTH EAST

CARTOON BOOKS
ON FOOT & FINGER
ON MORE FEET & FINGERS
LAUGHS ALONG THE PENNINE WAY

*Also a full range of guidebooks
to walking, scrambling, ice-climbing,
rock climbing, and other adventurous
pursuits in Britain and abroad*

---

*Other guides are constantly being added to the Cicerone List.
Available from bookshops, outdoor equipment shops or direct (send for price list)
from CICERONE, 2 POLICE SQUARE, MILNTHORPE, CUMBRIA, LA7 7PY*

Printed by CARNMOR PRINT & DESIGN,
95-97 LONDON ROAD, PRESTON, LANCASHIRE, UK.